ESSAY WRITING MADE EASY

Presenting Ideas in all Subject Areas

Ann Birch

Pembroke Publishers Limited

© 1993 Pembroke Publishers
   538 Hood Road
   Markham, Ontario L3R 3K9

Canadian Cataloguing in Publication Data

Birch, Ann
   Essay writing made easy

Includes bibliographical references and index.
ISBN 1-55138-016-1

1. English language – Rhetoric. 2. Report writing.
I. Title.

PE1471.B57 1993   808'.042   C93-094731-2

Contributing Editor: John Birch
Editor: Evlyn Windross
Design: John Zehethofer
Typesetting: Jay Tee Graphics Ltd.

This book was produced with the generous assistance of the government
of Ontario through the Ministry of Culture and Communications.

Printed and bound in Canada by Webcom
9 8 7 6 5 4 3 2

CONTENTS

INTRODUCTION

If you are an average student, you probably look on essay-writing as a disagreeable activity, like cleaning your room or supervising your little brother's Cub group on an excursion to the zoo. You may be surprised to know that many adults find writing difficult, too. Margaret Laurence said that she often cleaned the house from top to bottom to give herself an excuse for not sitting down at her typewriter. Another writer, Walter R. Smith, puts it more dramatically: "Writing is simple; I just sit down at the typewriter and open a vein."

Essay writing may be one of the simpler ways for a beginner to ease into the creative process. In the hands of a skilled professional, like Lance Morrow, Charlotte Gray, Russell Baker, or Allan Fotheringham, the essay becomes a highly polished art form. But the essay has a simple basic structure that even the most unpractised writer can easily learn.

It is essential to master this structure because over the course of your educational career you will probably write dozens of essays. In high school, community college, or university, you will use the essay to express what you know, think, and feel. Often, your essays will prove to others that you have the communication skills necessary for success in today's competitive world. Many universities now ask applicants to write a short essay giving their reasons for wanting to get into a certain program.

This book will teach you how to build a good essay. It will also offer suggestions on where to get ideas, how to use the library and how to revise and polish your work. I hope it will help you to write with confidence and skill.

ACKNOWLEDGEMENTS

I wish to thank the many students who provided examples of good writing for this book.

I also am grateful to the following professional writers who allowed their material to be used:

Barbara Amiel, for the excerpt from "The courage of the bike rider," from the July 31, 1989 issue of *Maclean's*, published by Maclean Hunter Canadian Publishing.

Fred Bruning, for the excerpt from "Black and white in America," from the June 1, 1992 issue of *Maclean's*, published by Maclean Hunter Canadian Publishing. Fred Bruning is on the staff of *Newsday* in New York and writes the monthly column, "An American Essay," for *Maclean's*.

Eliza Clark, for the paragraph from her novel *Miss You Like Crazy*, published by Coach House Press.

Bruce Obee, for the excerpt from "Defender of the bald eagle," in the March/April 1993 issue of *Canadian Geographic*.

Suzanne Zwarun, for the excerpt from "Why are judges so lenient in sexual assault cases?" in the September 1988 issue of *Chatelaine*.

I also thank my sons John and Hugh and my editor Evlyn Windross for their advice, encouragement, and contributions.

1

LOOKING AT ESSAY MODELS

Defining an Essay

The word "essay" means simply "an attempt." You write an essay when you are attempting to explain ideas. While there are many kinds of essays — literary essays, research essays, persuasive essays, to name a few — they all have one thing in common: they make a point about the topic you are discussing. In an essay, you present an opinion (called your thesis) and go on to provide supporting evidence for it. Essays are one of the best ways to demonstrate and share what you have learned and what you know and believe.

Following are three examples of different types of essays. Two of them were written by students like yourself. Though they all have the same basic structure (a beginning, middle and end) and all present a thesis, their approach and language vary according to their audience (the people reading them) and specific purpose.

Note: See the Appendix, page 85, for other types of essays and related forms: the research essay, the examination essay, the review, and the research report.

The Personal Essay

AUDIENCE

- usually a wide audience; perhaps your teacher, members of your class, students and parents who read your school magazine or newspaper, or the judges in a contest to which you are submitting your essay.

- to make a point in an entertaining or challenging way, by giving examples from personal experience.

LANGUAGE

- usually conversational and informal.
- may contain first-person pronouns like "I," "me," "we," or "us."

COMMENT

This essay appeared in a school literary magazine. At first glance, it may seem to be simply a charming story rather than an essay. But you will notice that the writer makes her point clear in paragraph three and again in the last sentence of her essay.

Another Saturday Night

by *Erin Woodley*

It's best if they don't live too far away from your house. Sure the car is most often nice, a Mercedes or a Jaguar, but the "Mr." usually smells of too much cologne and he doesn't say much, just sings along (under his breath, of course) to the music on the stereo.

The house is spotless and the children clamber around "Mom" in all her finery. I am a regular at this station so "Mom" just waves a hand at the fridge where the necessary phone numbers are posted, and dutifully kisses each child on the forehead. As she makes her escape out the front door, she turns and wags a finger at her beautiful children, "Be good for Erin now, and remember, bedtime is eight o'clock. Goodnight."

Well I'm free at last. The parents are gone and I can do what I want, right? Wrong. As a babysitter I am supposed to be here for the children. I am now their personal slave, playmate, snack-maker, bedtime-story reader and tucker-inner.

Like every other time I have been here, it takes the kids a few minutes to get comfortable around me again. They stare at me like I am some alien from outer-space; I ignore them and watch the TV. Eventually I feel a tug on my right earring, and a surprisingly loud voice suddenly shrieks, "Oh, I just looove your earrings! Can I wear them? Pleeaase." I shake my head, but before the inevitable tears, I cleverly change the subject and ask what movie they want to watch, *Bambi* or *Cinderella*? Oh no. They can't decide. It's too big of a decision. I can see the torment on their small pudgy faces. Their eyes shift from tape to tape. *Cinderella*? or *Bambi*? *Cinderella*? or ... I can't take it any more and decide that *Bambi* is the lesser of the evils, since I have seen it only three times.

I've timed it perfectly. The movie finishes at exactly quarter to eight, just enough time for milk and cookies before bed. One of the children, however, has his own idea, and standing straight in front of the television set he simply states "Cinda-rella." I tell him to hurry up and come into the kitchen if he wants a cookie. Wrong thing to say. "Cinda-rella! Cinda-rella! Cinda-rellllaaaa!" The kid is screaming at the top of his lungs. His sister is loving it. She just sits back on the sofa and watches. Being the wonderful babysitter that I am, after trying to reason with the little brat and getting nowhere, I follow my gut instinct and go for my bag-o-bribes. Let's see what I've got in here: Hubba Bubba Gum. Yeah, that'll do the trick.

It works like a charm. Twenty minutes later, I've got them both in bed. The only problem is they both still have a mouthful of the slimy Hubba Bubba. Oh how I would love to tell them that if they don't spit it out, they will choke and die and go to hell, but that would be totally against all rules in *The Good Babysitter's Handbook*, so instead I tell them that I just might bring them something better next time if they spit the gum out and go to sleep. The greedy little monsters think about my proposition for only a second before they both spit their oozing wads of pink Hubba Bubba into my outstretched palm. Gross.

Ten minutes later I am safe and sound downstairs. I've got a television, VCR, stereo, telephone, and a kitchen full of exotic foods like chocolate-raspberry-swirl ice-cream and cheddar cheese-flavoured potato chips. This is definitely what babysitting is all about.

———

AUDIENCE

- varies. Often people who have different opinions from the writer will read persuasive essays. The writer's challenge is to anticipate their arguments and try to change their ideas. I enjoyed this essay when I read it in a school magazine because it changed my views about cheerleaders.

PURPOSE

- to stimulate controversy, to persuade, and to change opinion.

LANGUAGE

- bold, pulls no punches.

COMMENT

Notice how this writer starts with the stereotypical view of cheerleaders and then spends the rest of her essay putting the record straight. This approach, which sets down the opposition's views and then blasts them to pieces, is an effective way of writing a persuasive essay.

It's Time to Put Women in their Place

by Agata Smoluch

Who do these girls think they are? Clad in tight sweaters, they wear skirts that barely cover their behinds. They bop around, their pony tails swinging to and fro. Shaking their pompoms, they lure men into their webs. They are an embarrassment to all modern women.

Cheerleaders have often been viewed as stupid, vain, and unathletic. They have even been shunnned for not participating in a "real sport." I think it's about time that we straighten out these theories.

If attaining honours is any indication of the level of intellect of an individual, last year's cheerleading team had 9 out of 13 girls on the honour roll. Those girls just squashed the first stereotype. And as far as being vain, I think most people are concerned with the way they look. But when the girls arrive at 7 a.m.

practices, they are far from preened.

Is cheerleading a sport? That's a question that's been tossed around for quite some time. Sport is defined as "any recreational activity; specifically, a game, competition, etc. requiring bodily exertion." Or as our phys. ed. teacher often says, "If you can smoke while you do it, it's not a sport."

To determine if cheerleading is a sport, we must look at what cheerleaders actually do. They scream, they wiggle, they giggle, and they put on make-up, right? Not exactly.

My day begins with a 6 a.m. alarm. After a quick shower and dressing regimen, I grab my blaster and I'm out the door. I make it just in time for the seven o'clock practice to begin. After a few laps around the gym and a brief aerobic warm-up, we're ready to start. Our first mission is "toe-touches." They require leaping vertically into the air while splitting our legs and touching our toes at the top of the jump. Easy, right? You try it, go on. Take a break from reading and try a toe-touch, and try lighting a cigarette while you're at it.

Now it's time for some wild and funky dancing! My favourite part. Have you ever tried dancing a choreographed routine over and over for an hour and a half? Well, guess what? You sweat! Yes, it's true; believe it or not, cheerleaders work hard and do indeed sweat.

By this time we've got to get to class and try to keep up those outstanding marks. But if it's Thursday, look forward to a three-hour stunting practice after school. "Stunting?" you ask. "What's that?" This is definitely the most complex part of cheerleading, both to perform and to explain. A stunt consists of one person in some form supporting another. For example, a liberty. Picture it: one girl is holding another girl above her head by the second girl's foot. Sound bizarre? Catch it at our next Thursday's practice.

Cheerleading isn't a sport. It's more than a sport. To be a successful cheerleader, the following attributes are a must. Coordination for all that dancing. Strength for lifting and throwing your friends around. Flexibility for the formidable toe-touch. Self-confidence for getting up in front of hundreds of fans with two minutes left and your team losing 32-0. Discipline for 7 a.m. practice four times a week. But most important, cheerleaders must have positive attitudes, be friendly but assertive, and demonstrate leadership and sportsmanship. Have you had a plateful yet?

If you ask me, cheerleading is a lot like volleyball. All you have to do is get the players to memorize every step they plan on taking. Then throw in some synchronized dancing, a few toe-touches, a 45-second cheer with motions, and some crowd-pleasing stunts. And don't forget to smile.

The Literary Essay

AUDIENCE

- usually your teacher or classmates. Often the audience will have read the work, so you must go beyond a plot summary to offer new insights.

PURPOSE

- to show that you have thought about one or several pieces of literature and to discuss your understanding of them.
- often to point out similarities, contrasts, or both among several pieces of literature.
- sometimes, to relate the world of literature to our world.

LANGUAGE

- formal, but keep it simple.

COMMENT

This essay connects three stories and fulfils all the purposes mentioned above. It tells the audience *briefly* about the plots of these tales in order to make a point, but doesn't retell the plot in detail. A literary essay must never be a plot summary.

Notice as well how this writer uses different paragraphs for each of the stories she is discussing, but pulls the stories together by careful links, usually in the first or second sentence of the paragraph.

Note also that this essay uses a footnote. A newer, easier method of documenting sources is now popular. You will find a discussion of both methods of documentation in Chapter 6.

Myths Help Us Understand Ourselves

by A. Birch

A young woman falls in love with a drug-dealer who pays for her first-class airfare to New York City for a romantic weekend. Her parents despair. Threats and removal of privileges have no effect. Eventually, she herself breaks off her relationship and starts a romance with a pleasant young law student whom her parents thoroughly approve of.

The literary critic, David Creighton, would say that the young woman in this story is acting out "the myth within."[1] She is going through the age-old process of revolt against authority figures (in this case, her parents) and choosing her own path in life, however disastrous. Creighton and other scholars contend that by studying myths — those important stories from the past about good and evil, about discipline and revolt, about death and rebirth — we come to understand ourselves better.

The story of Phaethon, an ancient myth from the Greek culture, gives us the archetype of revolt. An archetype is simply a model for repeated events and patterns which occur again and again in literature and in life. Phaethon's revolt takes the form of disobedience of the wishes of Apollo, the sun god. The young man thinks that he can drive the god's chariot across the heavens. Apollo knows that Phaethon is too inexperienced, but he eventually weakens and gives in. Phaethon soon finds himself unable to control the horses. He plunges to earth with the chariot, setting the world on fire, and getting himself killed in the process. Thousands of young people recreate this archetype every Saturday night when they badger their parents into handing over the keys of the family car. Often their story does not end tragically, as does Phaethon's, but the principle of revolt against the wishes of the authority figure is exactly the same.

Of course every child is familiar with the story of "Little Red Riding Hood," a folktale centred around the archetype of revolt. The little girl's rebellion is just like that of the young woman who gets involved with the drug-dealer. In the folktale the girl goes off in her red cloak (red is the archetypal colour of revolt), meets

---

[1] <u>Myths Within</u> (Toronto: Gage Educational Publishing Company, 1992) 1.

a wolf, and strikes up a conversation with him in defiance of her mother's advice. The rest of the story is well known: the wolf does some very nasty things in the bedroom of her grandmother's house, frightening Little Red Riding Hood badly. In the end she is rescued by a handsome woodsman who is really another version of the law student. Red Riding Hood's grandmother signals her approval of this young man by inviting him in for a lunch of fruit and milk (both archetypal symbols of fertility).

By reading myths and folktales, we can put our own lives in perspective. The parents of the girl who had the romance with the drug-dealing villain will understand that revolt by the young is a necessary and inevitable part of the testing and experimenting that go along with the growth process.

2

RESEARCHING YOUR TOPIC

Limiting Your Topic

Sometimes you will have a specific essay topic to write about; for example, "The Young Offenders' Act ignores the rights of the victims of youthful criminals." When you get a very defined topic like this one, you have a clear direction to go in.

But more likely, your teacher will give very general topics. Or you may have in your own mind a subject area in which you would like to do an independent study. In such cases, you may have broad ideas like these to start with:

Japanese internment during World War II
the relationship between Canadian art and Canadian literature
rights of indigenous peoples
drug and alcohol abuse
pollution
food additives
racism in our schools
equality in the workplace

Most of your high school essays will be relatively short, probably not more than 1200 words or about four or five typed, double-spaced pages. Therefore, topics like the above ones are far too general for you to deal with in so short a space. Each of them might require a full book to do justice to the topic.

Your first step, therefore, is to choose a corner of the subject to explore in detail. To do this, you can often rely on your own wits, especially if you choose a subject that you already have some knowledge of. Let's take, for example, the general topic "Pollution." You can easily subdivide this broad topic into smaller ones, by using a web or jotting down questions. For example:

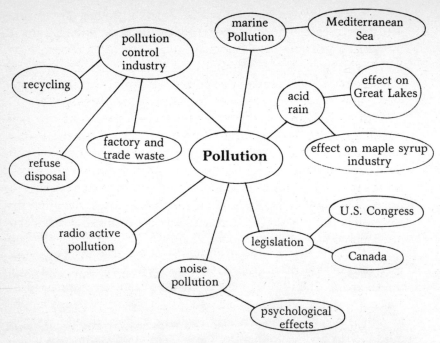

You could probably find, without difficulty, at least ten other areas of pollution to explore. Your final choice might depend on what you were interested in and what could be easily researched.

Using a Variety of Sources

You will find a variety of sources of information on almost any topic you pick. Each source will give you a slightly different viewpoint on your subject. Reference books supply general information. Magazine and news articles may give you more recent data. Interviews, biographies, and personality profiles provide a personal view. Surveys can tap the opinions of ordinary people.

Remember, too, that you will have your own point of view on a topic. Sometimes you may have very strong opinions on controversial issues. In your research, you may be tempted to look only at books and articles which support your own views. But make sure that you examine opposing ideas as well in order to get a balanced and accurate perspective on your subject.

Following are some information sources to consider.

Tapping Human Resources

Your own experience

Events in your own life often provide solid ground on which to build your essay. Many experiences would be suitable for an informal personal essay. For example, if you are a recent immigrant who has experienced racism in the cafeteria, corridors, or classrooms of your school, you could write a convincing personal essay about your experiences for your school newspaper.

With an informal personal essay, the approach may be serious or amusing. For example, if your topic is personal responsibility for a safe, healthy environment, you might draw on your own experiences as part of a volunteer youth group who cleaned up the ravine behind your school. A serious approach to the topic might show how the garbage along the ravine poses a health threat to small children playing there and to wild animals. A humorous approach could present the viewpoint of an archaeologist from the year 2300. From your experience in picking up beer cans, hamburger cartons, and other debris along the ravine, you could comment on what society in the 1990s must have been like.

Even if you are doing a research essay instead of a personal one, you may still use your own experience to provide valuable information. For example, your after-school job with a major fast-food franchise might give you inside knowledge about waste, which you could use in an essay on the need for recycling programs.

Interviews with experts

One of the best ways to get information is from interviews with people who have inside knowledge about your topic. Interviews with these people will give your essay a freshness which is lacking if you get all your information from books, magazines, and newspapers.

Experts do not have to be well-known people. Often ordinary people have viewpoints that are valid and forceful. Indeed, your friends, neighbours, and relatives may be the very people whose ideas will give your essay richness and relevance.

Suppose, for example, that you are investigating the care of old people in provincial or state nursing homes. You may have a grandmother who lives in one of these homes. Get her to talk about her experiences as a patient. She may have friends in the home who would be willing to talk to you as well. Several interviews of this nature would provide solid first-hand information for your topic.

You will probably find it easy to interview people you know. But there are times when you may want to interview strangers. To give yourself confidence and to make the best use of interview time, follow these suggestions.

INTERVIEW TIPS

Setting Up the Interview

- Arrange the interview in advance by telephone. Introduce yourself and explain what you are doing. For example: "I'm Jane Collett. I'm investigating the safety of our drinking water for an essay I'm writing. Is there someone there at Greenpeace who would be willing to give me an interview?"

Preparing for the Interview

- Do some reading in advance so that you know something about the topic. Try to get information about the person you are interviewing.
- Prepare your questions in advance and make sure that they are clear.
- Dress conservatively. It's not the time to wear your L.A. Raiders T-shirt and back-to-front baseball cap.

Getting a Successful Interview

- Be punctual and courteous.
- Open the interview with something of real interest to the interviewee and then let her talk. Your opening question should stimulate ideas.
- Be flexible. If the person you're interviewing strays into an interesting area, go along with him, rather than sticking rigidly to your prepared questions. You can always get back on track later.
- Ask open-ended questions, rather than those that call for a "yes" or "no" answer. Encourage discussion. It's better to ask, "What would be the best way to clean up Lake Erie?" than "Would you impose a fine on industrial polluters?"
- Note details of setting and personality that may be worked into your essay. Try taking mental pictures for the reader as you talk to your interviewee: general appearance, characteristic

gestures or expressions, quality of voice. Are there any items that help give you insight into her personality?
- Listen carefully and consider your interviewee's answers in order to make certain that you understand him and correctly interpret his meaning.
- Be careful about information given you in confidence. Your interviewee will probably tell you when his statements are "off the record." Be careful also not to print any information given in personal conversation. By taking out your notebook or by turning on your tape recorder, you signal to your interviewee that the interview has begun.

Taking Notes
- Don't attempt to keep a complete record of everything that is said during the interview. Select key words and phrases that will help you reconstruct the interview later.
- If you want to use a tape recorder, always ask permission first. Many people prefer not to have everything they say recorded.

Following-up
- Go over your notes or tape right after the interview. The longer you wait, the harder they will be to figure out. Get the substance of the interview into your essay while you still have a vivid memory of it.
- Finally, write a brief, courteous thank-you note to your interviewee.

Requesting Information by letter

If the person you want to interview lives out of town, you will probably have to get your information by letter. Keep your request short and simple. People may receive several requests for information every day, and they cannot take large amounts of time out of their schedules to respond. Ask one question which is most important to you, and enclose a stamped self-addressed envelope to make it easy and inexpensive for them to reply.

Surveys

Surveys are useful to get an informal sampling of opinion from a number of people, rather than an in-depth view from a few people. The results may even change your mind about your subject. One of my senior students, for example, was writing an essay on the reading habits of first-year students in our school. Because he did not like reading himself, he assumed that most students felt the way he did about books. He was surprised to find, when he completed his survey, that 80% of the students enjoyed reading and in fact read regularly for fun and information.

Survey Tips

- Get permission, especially if the subject matter is controversial.
- State the purpose at the top of the page. For example: "This survey is to determine reasons for vandalism of school property."
- Indicate that answers are confidential.
- Give a deadline for the return and a location to which to send it.
- Thank the participants for their time.
- Keyboard your survey. People don't want to read messy handwriting.
- Follow the suggestions below for writing questions.

Dos and Don'ts for Survey Questions

✓ DO be sure you word your questions clearly. For example, the question "Would you date a person from another culture?" is unclear. To some, it might mean "Would you date a person from another country?" To others, it might mean "If I am black, would I date a white person?"

✓ DO try your questions on a few people before you make a final draft of your survey. You will be able to see if they had trouble understanding your questions or answering them. This precaution will save you getting back 500 completed surveys with answers that are incomplete or misdirected.

x DON'T show biases or prejudices in your questions. For example, "Do you feel that our government should stop letting in immigrants because they take jobs away from citizens of our country?" shows bias against immigrants. Instead, you might ask a neutral question. For example, "Do you agree with our government's present immigration policies?"

x DON'T make assumptions. For example, "How do you feel when someone makes a racial slur against you?" assumes that the person has had this experience. Two questions could be asked: "Have you ever had someone make a racial slur against you?" Yes _____ No _____

"If you answered 'yes,' how did you feel?"

x DON'T ask two questions rolled into one. For example, "Would you marry someone of a different colour and religion?"

✔ DO ask one open-ended question at the end of your survey if you want an interesting quotation that you can use in your essay. For example: "Stating your reasons, tell whether or not you feel that there is racial harmony in our school."

The Library or Resource Centre

Is the library a strange land or familiar territory for you?

Some of you are very much at home in a library. You already know how to use its resources and feel comfortable in it. You can skip this part of the book if you know all about the card catalogue, microfiche, the computer catalogue, CD-ROM, vertical files, special encyclopedias, and the periodical indexes. Good for you!

But if you feel like a stranger in a strange land when you enter a library, read on!

Getting started

To give you confidence in using the library and to help you get started independently on your research, take some time to orient yourself. Locate the things you will eventually need for your research: the card catalogue (a number of little file trays in large metal or wooden cabinets usually located near the entrance); the computer terminals; the vertical files (usually in filing cabinets with large drawers); and the section where the reference books are stored. Take some time to look around in each of these areas to get an idea of what information you might get from them.

If you want to ask for help, try to keep your questions specific. "Will you show me how to use the microfiche viewer, please?" Remember, librarians just don't have time to teach you all the basics of library use on a busy Saturday.

You are now ready to research the information you need for your essay.

The Card Catalogue

If you want to know what books are available on your subject, first consult the card catalogue. (Some libraries have replaced the card catalogue with computers and microfiche because they are easier to keep up to date.)

If you have no definite book titles or names of authors in mind, try looking under the subject. For example, suppose you are doing an essay on the safety of the drinking water from Lake Ontario. You might look in the card catalogue under the general subject heading POLLUTION, or perhaps GREAT LAKES. Don't expect to find an exact narrowed subject area which corresponds with your topic. You would probably not find a subject card entitled SAFETY OF DRINKING WATER IN LAKE ONTARIO.

Here's what you might find when you check out the subject POLLUTION in a card catalogue in a small library.

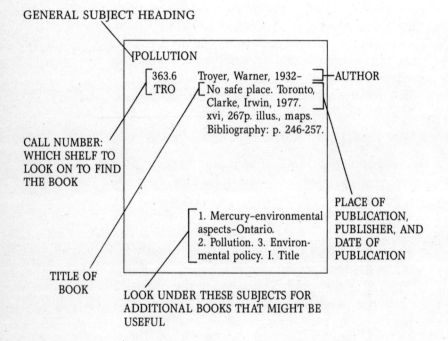

GENERAL SUBJECT HEADING

POLLUTION

363.6   Troyer, Warner, 1932– —AUTHOR
TRO   No safe place. Toronto,
     Clarke, Irwin, 1977.
     xvi, 267p. illus., maps.
     Bibliography: p. 246-257.

CALL NUMBER:
WHICH SHELF TO
LOOK ON TO FIND
THE BOOK

1. Mercury-environmental
aspects–Ontario.
2. Pollution. 3. Environ-
mental policy. I. Title

PLACE OF
PUBLICATION,
PUBLISHER, AND
DATE OF
PUBLICATION

TITLE OF
BOOK

LOOK UNDER THESE SUBJECTS FOR
ADDITIONAL BOOKS THAT MIGHT BE
USEFUL

Microfiche

If your library has microfiche, it may give you additional information on books available on your subject. Microfiche is a way of reducing hundreds of pages of book listings onto one 5″ x 4″ plastic slide. You must use a viewer to see the information on it. The slides are arranged alphabetically under broad subject areas like ABORTION or DRUG USE or INSURANCE. The librarian can show you how to use this simple form of catalogue.

Computer

Another method of finding books is through a computer search. Each library has a slightly different system which the librarian can explain to you. Or follow the instructions normally posted near the computer terminal or on the screen. Most systems involve keying in the subject you are interested in. For example, by keying in the word POLLUTION you will see the listings of books which the library has on the subject. The computer may also suggest additional subject headings under which you can look for information. For example, it may tell you to look under WATER MANAGEMENT or WATER POLLUTION.

Locating Books

Whether you are using the card catalogue, microfiche, or the computer, be sure to copy down the titles, authors, and call numbers (the area of the library in which you will find the books). For example, from the card catalogue entry shown in this chapter, you would write down on a note-pad:

Troyer, Warner (last name and first name of author);
No safe place (title of book);
363.6 TRO (call number of book).

Using the call numbers to get you to the right place, you locate your books next. You will usually find the general call number of your area displayed clearly on the side of the bookshelves or above: 300, for example. Once you have found what you need, look around in the same section. Possibly there will be other books on the shelf that may be useful to you.

Periodical and News Indexes

If you have a "hot" topic, one that is very much in the news at the moment, you will want to look at current magazines and newspapers.

For example, if you are researching job opportunities for the current year's high school graduates, you will not find this information in book form. Similarly, if you are writing on the effects of the newest video games on the mental and physical health of players, you may have a hard time finding a book that will deal with the very latest video technology. In situations like these, newspapers and magazines will provide information that has not yet been published in books.

To search out articles that may help you make your essay really up to date and relevant, you need to know about several important indexes. You will find these indexes in the reference section of the library. Once you have found the names of promising articles on your subject in these indexes, the librarian will locate the magazine or newspaper for you. Old copies of newspapers are kept on rolls of microfilm which you can look at on a machine called a reader.

a) THE CANADIAN PERIODICAL INDEX: Published monthly, it lists all the articles on your subject which have been written in Canadian and major American magazines. It does not include newspapers.

Here is a typical entry under the subject heading WATER POLLUTION:

> Toxins, toxins everywhere: the Great Lakes reel under an invisible assault. il. <u>Newsweek</u> 112 no 5 (Ag 1'88): p48

Here's how you decode this entry. On page 48 of the August 1, 1988 issue of *Newsweek*, you will find an article entitled "Toxins, toxins everywhere: the Great Lakes reel under an invisible assault." The short form "il." means that there is an illustration with the article, and "112 no 5" refers to the volume and the number of the issue.

Once you have copied down the information from the entry, give it to the librarian who will help you find the magazine.

b) THE READERS' GUIDE TO PERIODICAL LITERATURE: It gives similar information but includes more American magazines. It does not give information on newspapers. Some libraries have a video which explains how to use this guide.

c) THE CANADIAN NEWS INDEX: This is where you find the newspaper articles that have been written on your subject. The news stories are taken from seven major Canadian newspapers from coast to coast.

If you are researching the topic of the safety of drinking water, for example, you turn first to the subject WATER POLLUTION. Here you find a sub-section called GREAT LAKES REGION. In this section, you look for an article which seems to be closely related to your essay topic.

You find the following:

Toxins make Ontario "dirtiest" of Great Lakes citizens' group warns
TS S 2 '88 pA3

By now, you are probably able to figure out most of this entry on your own. "TS" means Toronto Star. "S 2 '88" refers to the September 2, 1988 edition of the paper where the article is located in Section A, page 3.

Copy down the information about the entry and go to the micro-film section of the library where the old newspapers are stored on rolls of film. The librarian will help you locate the right roll and show you how to use the reading machine. If your library does not have microfilm facilities, you may be able to request a copy of the article from another library.

d) HISTORICAL ABSTRACTS: "Abstracts" are summaries. This index includes summaries of articles from 2,000 journals relating to all areas of the world, except for the United States and Canada. The best approach is to look under the subject indexes at the end of each volume. For example, you would find many abstracts of articles on a popular subject like "Emigration."

e) PUBLIC AFFAIRS INFORMATION SERVICE BULLETIN: This useful index provides a list of articles, books, and government publications from around the world on public policy and public affairs. It covers the fields of economics, political science, business, sociology, law, and education.

The Vertical File

The vertical file is a collection of clippings or photocopies from newspapers and magazines covering common topics that the average reader might want to know more about. These clippings are stored in subject folders in large filing cabinets.

Sometimes the vertical file is helpful; sometimes it is not. Often the list of subjects on which it gives information is rather limited. If you are lucky enough to find a vertical file on your subject, however, you will have a lot of useful information collected in one place for you.

The Social Issues Resources Series (SIRS)

Better than the vertical file, this resource is a series of loose-leaf binders on popular social, environmental, and historical subjects.

Usually located near the reference section of the library, these binders contain articles from (mainly) American newspapers and magazines on a variety of popular topics; for example, alcoholism, aging, abuse of the elderly, the world wars, and the environment. *SIRS* also has articles on important people in the news.

The Opposing Viewpoints Series

This series is useful for researching both sides of a current social issue; for example, abortion and capital punishment. There is a *Junior* series for students whose English language skills are limited.

Special Encyclopedias and Reference Books

If you have an essay topic which you know very little about, the first place you may want to look is in the reference section of the library. Here you will find general reference books which will help you get started.

Already you are probably familiar with general encyclopedias like *The New Encyclopaedia Britannica* and *The World Book*. But are you aware of the many special encyclopedias which can help you with a particular subject area? There is an encyclopedia, dictionary, or guide on practically everything under the sun.

Here are just a few of the hundreds of helpful reference books that you might find on the shelves of any library:

Benet's Reader's Encyclopedia
A Dictionary of Canadian Artists
Encyclopedia of Human Behaviour: Psychology, Psychiatry, and Mental Health
Encyclopedia of Pop, Rock, and Soul
Encyclopedia of Psychology
Encyclopedia of Visual Art: Volume I — A History of Art Volume 2 — A Biographical Dictionary of Artists
McGraw-Hill Encyclopedia of Science and Technology
Reader's Guide to Canadian History

Often reference books will give you hints on useful books to consult for further information of your essay topic. For instance, the section on ABORTION in *The Canadian Encyclopedia* highlights some of the legal and moral aspects of the subject, and then refers the reader to a 1986 book called *The Bedroom and the State*.

Audio-Visual Materials

Most libraries have a stock of tapes, records, filmstrips, and films. If they don't have what you need, the librarians can get it from other branches. Large school boards have a resource centre from which students can borrow audio-visual materials. Your teacher may have a catalogue showing what is available. Film distributors also offer a variety of catalogues.

CD-ROM

CD-ROM, short for Compact Disc—Read Only Memory, has revolutionized research by putting thousands of pages of information onto a single compact disc, much like those on which pre-recorded music is stored. For example, one disc has enough capacity to hold the entire 60 million words found in the 20-volume Second Edition of the *Oxford English Dictionary*, or the complete text of one year's issues of a major newspaper.

CD-ROM is basically a replacement for periodical indexes, encyclopedias, newspapers, magazines, and dictionaries. It allows the user to search for information in many more ways than would otherwise be possible. For example, the *Canadian News Index* catalogues major stories in only two ways: by author and by subject. But the CD-ROM version of the *Globe and Mail* (one of the publications catalogued by the *Canadian News Index*) is much more versatile. It allows you to search through all the stories by author, subject, keyword, date, or even a name (or word) mentioned in the text. What's more, the CD-ROM version carries the entire text of the story; you can find the article and read it in one step, instead of having to use an index and then track down the cited article on microfilm. If you decide that the article is valuable, you can even ask the computer to print it out on paper.

Using CD-ROM is easy, especially after you have done it several times. To access the wealth of information, you just have to use the disc in a computer equipped with a CD-ROM reader and follow the instructions given by the software. Although the features vary somewhat, most discs generally have the ability to search by subject, author, or word in text. You can also browse sequentially from article to article, much as you would if you were flipping through a book, newspaper, or encyclopedia. The software that comes with each disc usually has very clear directions about which keys to press to perform the search.

With CD-ROM, as with all research sources, you should be certain that you know exactly what you are looking for before you begin your search. If you want to know about the various ways that doctors treat breast cancer, it may be a great waste of time to look for everything about "cancer" because there may be hundreds of articles about lung cancer, skin cancer, and prostate cancer on the disc which will be of no use to you. Searching for the subject of "breast cancer" will therefore help you to find more relevant information.

Remember, too, that there are usually different ways in which you can structure your search in order to find the information that you need. If you are looking for an obscure topic, or if repeated subject searches yield nothing useful, then it may be worthwhile to perform a global search. A global search (also called a full-text search) looks at every word on the entire disc to see if any matches the word(s) which you are looking for. (It may take the computer up to several minutes to scan the whole disc and report the results to you.) By doing a full-text search, you will be able to pick out references to your topic, even when a full article is not devoted to the subject. Thus, you may find a profile of the pop music group "Crash Test Dummies" in a general article about the vitality of the national music scene. You may also find a mention of Marshall McLuhan in a piece about the influence of the media. It is extremely unlikely that you could have found these references using traditional indexes, but thanks to CD-ROM they are within easy reach of the researcher.

Users should remember that there are thousands of different CD-ROM discs available. While a well-stocked school library may own only a handful of different discs, a large public library may have hundreds, covering different areas such as science, business, politics, history, language, and current affairs.

To give you an idea of the range of CD-ROM materials being published, here is a very brief list of examples:

Business Periodicals OnDisc
CCINFOdisc (health and safety-related information about chemicals and pesticides)
Compact Disclosure (annual reports and financial data for 6,500 Canadian companies)
CDCS (an index to all U.S. federal government documents)

Dataworld Infodisk (full-text reports, charts and summaries covering computer hardware and software)

Dialog on Disc: Canadian Business and Current Affairs (gives listings of articles in Canadian newspapers and journals)

Grolier: The Electronic Encyclopedia

Index to United Nations Documents and Publications

McGraw-Hill Science and Technical Reference Set

Medline (comprehensive coverage of the primary journal literature in the biomedical sciences)

Oxford English Dictionary

Unity Disc: Canadian Confederation Issues and Opinions From Canadian News Sources, 1985-1991

Note-taking from Library Material

Scanning for Information

You will soon look like the Hunchback of Notre Dame if you lug home from the library everything you find on your topic. Take a few minutes at a table to look over your material and decide what will be useful.

In magazines and news articles, captions under pictures and headings on each section of the article provide clues to the content. With books, look at the table of contents and the index to see how much useful information there is.

Recording Sources

If you always tell where the information in your essay comes from, no one will accuse you of plagiarism, which means stealing someone else's ideas and passing them off as your own. Therefore, you must do one important thing before beginning your note-taking, and that is to record essential details about your information sources.

On large index cards or sheets of paper — one for each book or article — write down the following information at the top.

FOR A BOOK

CALL NUMBER	330 A
AUTHOR	Archer, Maurice
TITLE	<u>Introduction to Economics: A Canadian</u> <u>Analysis, Second Edition</u>
PLACE OF PUBLICATION	Oakville, Ontario
PUBLISHER	Maurice Archer Enterprises
DATE OF PUBLICATION	1984

FOR AN ARTICLE

AUTHOR	Laver, Ross
TITLE (in quotation marks)	"The debate about life"
NAME OF NEWSPAPER OR MAGAZINE	Maclean's
DATE OF ISSUE	July 31, 1989
PAGE NUMBER	Page 20

Use the space left on each card or page for the notes you make from the book or article. Be sure to record the exact page numbers of quotations or of points that you summarize in your own words. If you follow this routine, you will find it easy to assemble your notes when you get to the point of actually writing your essay.

Making Notes Effectively

Note-taking is like eating an Oreo. Although the outside layers taste fine, you want to suck out the soft, squishy centre that is the essence of the cookie. Like Oreos, most articles or chapters in a book have a basic structure. Once you know this structure it is easy to find the essence.

Here are some tips for extracting the essence of most articles.

NOTE-TAKING TIPS

- Scan titles, headings, and captions to get a basic idea about the content.
- Look for the THESIS. This is a statement or question that provides the real centre of what the article is about. It often comes somewhere in the first, second, or third paragraph of an article or chapter.
- Go through the rest of the chapter or article looking for TOPIC SENTENCES. These are sentences, usually found near the beginning of each paragraph, that summarize the topic that the author will be discussing in the rest of the paragraph. Topic sentences will show you whether the rest of the paragraph will be useful for your essay or not.
- Look for KEY WORDS within each paragraph that signal important ideas. For example, words like "some" and "others" may alert you to look for two opposing viewpoints.
- Always scan the last paragraph or CONCLUSION of an article or chapter. Here the writer will often summarize or restate the main points.
- Try to PARAPHRASE the author's ideas; that is, put them in your own words. Use exact quotations only when they seem especially persuasive, concise, or memorable.

Remember, the essay you are writing is your own. It should give *your* viewpoint and not be just a rehash of someone else's opinions. When you see something that you disagree with or that you want more information about, put your thoughts down in the notes, but indicate clearly that they are *your own*. Some students put their initials besides their comments so that they don't get them mixed up with those of the writer whose article they are summarizing. Another method of separating your own ideas is to use a highlighter or square brackets. For example, note-taking from an article on abortion might appear like this:

> Benjamin Freedman feels that we have a moral obligation to protect a fetus which can live outside the uterus. [Mmm — not sure if I agree. What about defective fetuses? What about pregnancy as a result of rape or incest?]

The process of questioning what you read and recording your own comments helps give you ownership over your essay.

3

PLANNING AND DRAFTING

Pre-writing

There is no clear-cut moment when you are ready to construct the first draft of your essay. When you've read about your topic, thought about it, talked about it, made your notes, and formed your own ideas about what you want to say, you'll reach a point where you are ready to begin your essay. You may want to get into your most comfortable sweat-shirt and make yourself a cup of coffee while you review the important concepts of audience and basic essay structure.

Considering Your Audience

Your audience influences what goes into your essay. In other words, who is going to be reading it? Your teacher only? Your classmates? Most of the students in your school? The judges in an essay competition you're entering? The people in your community?

For example, let's see how different audiences would determine the content of a literary essay on *The Merchant of Venice*. If you were writing this essay for classmates who had studied the play, you would not need to tell them the plot. If, however, you were writing for your school's literary magazine, you might want to give a brief plot outline for those readers who have no knowledge of the play. Again, if you were attending a school with a large Jewish student population, you might plan to comment on the charge that the play is racist.

Basic Essay Structure

Having considered your audience, take a few minutes to review the basic structure of an essay. Not all essays stick to the following format, of course, but the pattern is one that a beginning writer will find easy to imitate.

BASIC ESSAY STRUCTURE

The Beginning

- The beginning of an essay consists of a *title*, a *hook*, and a *thesis*.
- The *title* points the reader towards your viewpoint on the topic. Often it is "catchy" as well. Example: Dead Leaves Spawn New Growth
- The *hook* snares your audience into reading your essay. It may be a striking comparison, a challenging quotation, a personal experience, or a controversial statement or statistic.
- The *thesis* is your viewpoint, which you set down as a result of thinking about and researching the topic.

  The hook and thesis paragraph of an essay on using dead leaves as bedding for worms might go something like this:

  > Each year in our city, thousands of uninformed home owners allow dead leaves to blow away or pack them into non-degradable plastic bags to linger for decades in land-fill sites. This ignorant waste of a valuable resource must stop. *(Hook)* Homeowners need to be aware that dead leaves provide a valuable home for worms, whose castings provide the rich nutrients for fertile soil. *(Thesis)*

The Middle

- The middle of an essay is a series of paragraphs, each with a topic sentence which develops the thesis. Here is a sample paragraph.

  A few simple precautions will turn dead leaves into an effective bedding for worms. *(Topic sentence: it refers back to the thesis and summarizes the information which follows in the rest of the paragraph.)* Choose leaves that have not been sprayed with chemicals. Remove noticeable insects. Then chop or shred the leaves before putting them into the vermi-composter box. The addition of peat moss will prevent the leaves from clumping together when you moisten them.

The End

- Endings to essays provide a brief summary, and often restate the thesis in a fresh and forceful way.

    Homeowners harvesting their tomato plants in mid-August will delight in the large, tasty, red fruit which comes from the rich compost provided by worms and those once-hated dead leaves.

Drafting a Working Thesis

Take time getting your thesis right. Although you may want to smooth and polish it later, it must be in place now because it is the basis of your entire essay structure.

Remember:

- A thesis is *your* viewpoint which you have come to as a result of researching and thinking about your topic.
- A thesis should offer a new perspective on the topic and not be just a rewriting of ideas that your audience has already heard many times.
- The thesis should be a statement that you can develop in some depth. If it is too broad, you cannot do justice to it.
- Most important of all, the thesis should provide a clear route into the rest of the essay. Inexperienced essay writers should use their thesis statements to mark out clearly the major parts of their essay.

These are examples of good student theses which map out the way to the middle of the essay:

> In pursuing excellence in sport, athletes should consider the following factors: avoiding injuries, adapting training to the needs of their particular sport, and keeping themselves motivated during training.

This essay will therefore have three sections in the middle: one on avoidance of injury, one on adaptation of training, and one on motivation.

Sweden's socialist state has greatly improved the quality of life through three successful means: the child-care programs, the youth development programs, and the industrial management schemes. The drawback to the first two is, of course, the high tax burden, but the last is largely funded by corporations and therefore imposes no burden on the tax payer.

The middle part of this essay is also clearly marked out. The writer will talk about child-care, youth development, and industrial management programs. He will then discuss the tax burden and finish off with details on the financing of the industrial schemes.

Building an Outline

Because these student theses have clearly marked sign-posts, they will be easy to make outlines for. An outline is necessary for your essay because it will remind you of the major points which you want to include.

Let's take the first thesis and show how an outline evolves easily from it.

ESSAY OUTLINE

The Beginning

Title: How to Reach Peak Form Safely, Successfully, and Happily
Hook: Perhaps a quotation from an Olympic gold medallist? A
  short anecdote from personal experience? (Decide later)
Thesis: In pursuing excellence in sport, athletes should consider
  the following factors: avoiding injuries, adapting training to the
  needs of their particular sport, and keeping themselves moti-
  vated during training.

The Middle

Part 1: Avoiding Injuries
  — Stretching exercises
  — Correct technique
  — Proper breathing
  — Back care
  — Pacing progress
Part 2: Adapting Training to the Needs of a Particular Sport
  — Weight training in the early stages
  — Determining the requirements for a particular sport
  e.g. baseball and golf — power

> cycling and racquet sports — muscular endurance
> skiing, football — power and muscular endurance
> — Determining the important muscles to develop for a
> particular sport
> Part 3: Keeping Motivation During Training
> — Use of a log to keep track of work-outs
> — Working with a partner
> — Use of music
> — Periodic competitions
>
> ## The End
>
> Quotation from Chicago White Sox catcher Carlton Fisk: "If the
> human body recognized agony and frustration, people would
> never run marathons, have babies, or play baseball."

You can see how easy it will be to draft an essay from this outline. An added benefit of an outline is that it can be used as a table of contents, by simply adding page numbers, if your teacher requires a table.

Writing the First Draft

It may be best to write quickly without agonizing over each word or phrase. You will revise later. At the start of the writing process, you need to fill up the pages and give yourself confidence that the essay is moving along.

E. B. White, the author of *Charlotte's Web*, used to say that when his wife Katharine was working on a book, "she would write eight or ten words, then draw her gun and shoot them down." Your own writing method may be like Katharine White's. If it is, that's all right. But most of you will want to move ahead rapidly with your first draft, following your outline and using your research notes to provide the information needed under each item.

You will notice that the sample outline does not spell out the details for the hook. Inspiration for it often comes later, during the revision process.

Note: Revisions are easy on a computer. If you are doing your first draft in hand-writing, however, write on every other line and on one side of the page only. You may want to use the back of the page later for major additions to your original draft.

4

TIPS FOR REVISING

Revising the First Draft

There is more to revising than simply copying out your first draft neatly or keyboarding it on your computer.

Revising is a process of making your essay as perfect as possible in its content and style so that it will be informative and interesting for your audience. Just as important in these days of fierce academic competition, it will earn you a good mark from your teacher.

If you revise properly, you may have to rewrite large chunks, switch paragraphs around, or even add extra details. One of the characters in a mystery story I've been reading — he is a journalist — says that writing consists mainly of pounding out words in the hope that some of them will actually be usable.

In revising your essay, you need to think of ways to start and end your essay effectively. You probably rushed through these parts in order to get on with your writing. You also need to look at your working thesis to see if it still applies to the ideas you have expressed. Sometimes ideas change and evolve as you write. Look, too, at your topic sentences and see if you have given enough supporting evidence to convince your readers of your main points. And finally, you should have someone you trust read your essay and give an opinion on it. This chapter will take you through these stages in revision.

Questions to Help You Revise

Revising involves reading your essay critically, to discover areas that may confuse a reader, or ways in which it can be improved. Use the following questions to help you revise effectively.

Do You Have a Good title?

The title is what catches the readers' eyes first and makes them decide to give your writing another glance. Think about essays in newspapers, for example. A recent essay on the gruesome mixture of crime and violence in children's television had the title "Saturday Morning Hell." It attracted my attention even though my children are no longer elementary school age. Yet it is amazing how many students hand in essays to their teachers with such titles as "Chemistry Assignment" or "Law Essay." No wonder the teacher decides that washing out the dog's dish might be a more interesting task than reading the essay!

Your title should give your reader an idea of your main topic and thesis. Looking at newspaper or magazine articles will give you suggestions of how professional writers use titles. For example, a recent essay had the title "Teenage Marriage: Long Days of Lonely Drudgery."

Be careful, though, not to use slangy, gimmicky titles on serious essays. Again, it's a matter of your audience, isn't it? While the teenage readers of the pop British magazine *Sky* might want to read a review essay on *Melrose Place* entitled "Another TV Show About Cute Babes and Studly Dudes," such a title would not be appropriate for a literary essay on *Romeo and Juliet* for your English teacher.

Is the Hook Effective?

If you think of the reader as a fish that you want to catch, then a tempting title will lure him towards your essay for a second or two, but a hook is the follow-up which will land him. Here are some good ways of hooking your reader.

NOTE: Many inexperienced writers use a dictionary definition as a hook. Experienced authors seldom use this type of hook. A dictionary definition is a boring way to start your essay. Using it shows that you don't care enough about your reader to find a really interesting and different way of hooking his attention.

EFFECTIVE "HOOKS"

- A striking METAPHOR or COMPARISON. A prize-winning student essay on the topic of racial harmony began this way: "Racial harmony could be compared to a series of musical chords that when played together produce a full and entertaining sound. But if one tried to play these chords separately they would sound empty and dull."
- A PERSONAL EXPERIENCE or an ANECDOTE to which the reader can relate. This method works well in the personal essay or in an essay dealing with social issues. For example, a student essay on the need for accurate consumer information about food additives began by briefly telling about a friend who suffered a severe allergy attack from the preservative sprayed over salads in a restaurant.
- A QUOTATION. Frequently, a quotation from a well-known person will give the beginning of your essay some credibility. For example, an essay on drug abuse in the music industry could start with a quotation from a rock star who is a reformed heroin addict.

If you are stuck for a quotation, you will find books of famous quotations on the library reference shelves.
- A CONTROVERSIAL STATEMENT, or a STARTLING STATISTIC. a random sampling of a national newspaper shows that professional writers often use this type of hook:
  — "Foreign nannies are often sitting ducks."
  — "Teen-aged dropouts are finding a fresh start where they least expected it — back in school."
- A RHETORICAL QUESTION. "Is the level of education deteriorating in North American schools? Is the school day becoming one lengthy spare period?" begins an essay in a recent school magazine. Rhetorical questions are the author's way of asking the reader to think about the central issues in the essay. Remember, though, that questions are the least used hook of professional writers, perhaps because they can sound forced and unnatural.

Is Your Thesis Statement Clear?

Does it
— reflect *your* viewpoint;
— offer a fresh, focused perspective on your topic;
— give a clearly marked route to the middle of your essay?

Try the following quiz as a way of testing your ideas about what makes a good thesis.

QUIZ

In each of the pairs, one thesis is satisfactory and one is unsatisfactory. See if you can pick the good ones.

1.a) Media guru Barry Duncan says that students need to be taught to look at television critically.

 b) Because television images of major politicians are so persuasive, students need to understand how television manipulates their voting response.

2.a) Mandatory instalment in cars of blood alcohol monitoring devices would reduce the number of tragedies caused by drunk drivers.

 b) Because of the suffering caused to the victims of drunk drivers, the government must impose stiffer penalties on people who drink and drive.

3.a) Recycling programs have saved regional governments millions of dollars.

 b) In one region, a recycling program by the local government has generated new income from secondary fibre markets, saved thousands of dollars in waste disposal fees, and created hundreds of new jobs.

4.a) Hamlet's tragic death is not the result of any failure in his character, as some critics insist, but the outcome of the moral rot in the Danish court.

 b) This essay will discuss the reasons for Hamlet's downfall.

ANSWERS

1.a) unsatisfactory: a spitting up of someone else's viewpoint.

 b) satisfactory: the writer has arrived at his own perspective on the need for a critical look at television coverage.

2.a) satisfactory: the writer has a fresh perspective.

 b) unsatisfactory: nothing new here; our response is a huge yawn.

3.a) unsatisfactory: too broad, too unfocused, unmanageable.

 b) satisfactory: gives a clear direction to the middle part of the essay; the writer will have no trouble organizing her material around three major advantages of recycling.

4.a) satisfactory: clear direction again; there will be several paragraphs looking at the viewpoints of "some critics" and refuting them, and several paragraphs explaining how the rottenness of the court leads to Hamlet's death.

 b) unsatisfactory: a lame beginning; no sign-posts to the middle of the essay.

Do Your Paragraphs Have Clear Topic Sentences and Supporting Details?

Remember that the purpose of the topic sentence is to tell your readers what the rest of the paragraph is about. It is always best for beginning writers to plant their topic sentences firmly at the beginning of their paragraphs and then use concrete details (examples, statistics, incidents, facts, and quotations) to build convincing evidence for the reader.

A couple of examples will illustrate this point more clearly. One student's history essay on the Crusades has the following thesis: "Though the Crusades cruelly depleted several generations of human beings, they had two outstanding benefits which led Europe into the Renaissance: they upset the entrenched feudal system, and they broadened and enriched the perceptions of narrow-minded Western Europeans."

Because this thesis is carefully laid out, the student has no difficulty in organizing the middle part of his essay into two distinct sections. Here is his topic sentence for the second section followed by the concrete details which convince his readers.

> The goods and knowledge brought back by the Crusaders as a result of their contact with the Byzantine and Muslim Empires greatly changed and often enriched their narrow, unsophisticated lifestyles. *(Topic sentence)* The Crusaders saw the wide roads, large windows, and working sewers in the Byzantine and Muslim empires and felt highly dissatisfied with their own constructions. *(Concrete detail No. 1)* In medicine, too, sick people found the Persian cures made from rose jam and spiced cream far more appealing than their own remedies of cat's grease and stewed slugs, though perhaps no more effective. *(Concrete detail No. 2)* As well, the knowledge of astronomy gained from the Persians let the Europeans navigate by the stars and thus find new lands to be explored. *(Concrete detail No. 3)* Sometimes, of course, the "improvements" were of dubious value. The introduction of the compass, gunpowder, and the printing press later helped the Spaniards to find new lands, utterly destroy them, and write fictionalized accounts of their valour. *(Concrete detail No. 4)*

Notice how another young writer develops her topic sentence with specific details. This paragraph is from a prize-winning essay which tells about how one remarkable teacher changed her attitude towards reading.

Each book we read was a new and exciting adventure. We read a funny book about a giant fish that lived in the sewer, and another about a blind shipwrecked boy who learned from an old white-haired man how to survive. My personal favourite is still so vivid in my mind that I can recall the title, *Tuck Everlasting*. This was a book about a family who had mistakenly drunk from a spring which made them live forever. Mrs. Al-Jbouri made the characters so real I can still see them in my mind, as though they are all really still alive.

The force of this paragraph comes from the details about the books. The paragraph would have less impact if she just talked vaguely about "funny," "exciting," or "adventure-packed" stories without specific comments about the plots and title of her favourites.

Short paragraphs are in style now. You will notice, if you look at essays in magazines, that paragraphs usually consist of no more than six sentences. Editors feel that people are likely to read articles if the paragraphs seem short and manageable. For research essays, paragraphs can be a little longer. As a general rule, though, keep your paragraphs to about half a page, double spaced.

Have You Linked Your Sentences and Paragraphs with Transitions?

If you neglect transitions, your essay will sound like something you wrote when you had a bad case of hiccups.

Here is an example of a student paragraph which has few transitions. You will notice that it has a choppy, disconnected effect.

What can we do to make our water safer to drink? We can update the 1940s technology at present being used in plants. We can crack down on industrial companies which dump 29 chemicals into our lake. We can avoid throwing solvents, dyes, polishes, and pesticides into the lake. Universal participation in a clean-up program is the only way to stop environmental disaster.

Here is the same paragraph rewritten with transitions (shown in italics):

What can we do to make our water safer to drink? *First*, we can update the 1940s technology at present being used in *water-treatment* plants. *Second*, we can crack down on industrial *polluters* who dump 29 *toxic* chemicals into our lake. *Finally, in our own homes*, we can avoid throwing solvents, dyes, polishes, and pesticides into our garbage *where they will end up leaking from dumps into our lake* for years to come. *Joint co-operation by industry and by private citizens* is the only way to stop environmental disaster.

You can see how the italicized transitions make the excellent concrete details flow together easily and convincingly.

Does Your Essay Have a Strong and Memorable Ending?

> This is the way the world ends
> This is the way the world ends
> This is the way the world ends
> Not with a bang but a whimper.
> T. S. Eliot

What T. S. Eliot says about the ending of the world is, alas, only too true of the endings of some student essays. Here are a few of the pitiful "whimpers" I've read lately:

— In conclusion, I have told you in this essay about the symbols in *The Glass Menagerie*.
— To sum up, the Young Offenders' Act needs something done about it.
— To conclude, Bertrand Russell was a great philosopher and I enjoyed his essay very much.

The best way to find out how to end with a "bang" is to look at the essays of professional writers in current magazines and newspapers. You will find that not one of them signals a conclusion with obvious phrases like "in conclusion," "to conclude," "I have shown you in this article," "therefore, it would seem that," "to sum up." And not one of them tells you what she has just done in the essay.

EFFECTIVE ENDINGS

Here are some professional strategies for ending an essay effectively:
• A QUOTATION, especially from some authority connected with the topic you are discussing. A *Canadian Geographic* article focuses on the damage caused to the bald eagle by lead pellets from shotgun shells. The article ends with a quotation from a crusading veterinarian about a bird he treated that died from badly damaged

kidneys. It was, he says, a "slow, inhumane, totally unnecessary death." Such a quotation not only gives human interest to the story, but also subtly emphasizes a major theme of the rest of the article.

• A QUESTION or a CHALLENGE. A well-known Canadian columnist, Barbara Amiel, writes in *Maclean's* about a 53-year-old motorcycle racer whose only ambition in life has been "to ride as fast as hell." Most readers probably find such an obsession a bit mad. But Amiel challenges our attitudes in her concluding paragraph:

> On July 5, at the Eastern Canadian championships at Shannonville, Ont., Frank Mrazek crashed into a wall. Bleeding and dazed, he dragged his bike back onto the course. He had to be pulled off the race track by the stewards. Crazy, you think? Then I wish I were too.

Sometimes the challenge to the reader can be in the form of a call to action. In a *Chatelaine* article which charges that judges are too lenient in sexual assault cases, the writer calls for women to make themselves responsible for change. Here is the last paragraph of the article:

> As women protest judicial decisions and remarks they think sexist. . .there will be changes in the legal yardstick of what constitutes rape. Then, judicial decisions will more fairly reflect the pain and terror felt by one in four Canadian women living today who will be sexually assaulted.

Of course, this writer has also used the device of shock in this conclusion as she slips into her last sentence that appalling statistic.

• A RETURN TO THE THESIS and a RESTATEMENT of it in an interesting way. Probably this is the most common way of concluding. Another issue of *Maclean's* contains an essay by Fred Bruning entitled "Black and white in America." His thesis is that the historical continuity of racism in the United States is the country's most fundamental problem. He gives as an example the race riots in Los Angeles.

The conclusion of this essay restates the thesis in these words:

> Defending a black man wrongly accused of murder more than a half-century ago, the renowned attorney Clarence Darrow told an all-white jury in Detroit that "the law has made the Negro equal, but man has not." Darrow challenged jurors to imagine themselves black, to purge themselves of rancor, to save

Detroit's reputation and their own. The defendant was acquitted, and for a moment, justice prevailed. Now comes Los Angeles, and another opportunity for Americans to salvage their reputations. We shall overcome, promises the old spiritual. For the sake of all, we better.

Getting Feedback

All writers, even professionals, need feedback from people they trust. You may have a friend, an older brother or sister, or parents who can read your essay and make suggestions. Or perhaps your class has peer editing groups that can look over your essay and offer comments.

You may want to get this feedback before you start your revisions. Or you may prefer to revise your essay at least once and then get suggestions from classmates and family for further improvements.

These readers can give valuable help by pointing out
— things that they like or find interesting in your essay;
— areas that seem unclear or confusing;
— information that seems unnecessary or repetitive;
— parts where they would like more details;
— obvious errors in spelling, punctuation, or grammar.

The following checklist may help your readers to focus on important areas in your essay. Or, you may use it to remind yourself of important areas to check.

It is not easy to take criticism. It is always painful to the ego to hear unpleasant truths. But remember, a person who takes time to point out areas in your essay that you could improve is a responsible, caring person who wants you to do well. It takes much less time, effort and courage for an evaluator simply to write "very good" on the top of the page. Such a comment, when you think about it, is virtually useless. Be grateful for a critic who evaluates your essay honestly and thoroughly.

It is, of course, up to you whether you want to make all the changes suggested by others. Probably you will find many of the comments helpful. But there may be areas where you want to leave things as they are.

REVISING CHECKLIST

- ☐ Does the title immediately grab your attention?
- ☐ Does the hook "hook" you?
- ☐ Is there a clear, focused thesis statement summarizing the writer's viewpoint?
- ☐ Is the information presented in the main part of the essay clearly understandable?
- ☐ Are the paragraphs developed with enough details?
- ☐ Are the facts and opinions presented in a lively manner?
- ☐ Has the writer done some original research: interviews, surveys, first-hand observation?
- ☐ Does the essay as a whole show the writer's viewpoint rather than just being a "rehash" of other people's opinions and ideas?
- ☐ Where the writer has used the opinions of others, has she/he been careful to give the source of these opinions?
- ☐ Is the essay appropriate for the audience for whom it was written?
- ☐ Is the conclusion strong and memorable?
- ☐ Are there obvious errors in spelling, grammar, punctuation, sentence structure, and diction?
- ☐ What are the strengths of this essay?
- ☐ How do you think it could be improved?

5

TIPS FOR EDITING

AND PROOFREADING

When you have spent time researching, thinking, and writing about your topic, you don't want your efforts to be spoiled by careless mistakes. Paying attention to your choice of language, spelling, punctuation, grammar, and sentence structure will give your essay that extra polish that is so important.

Here is some advice on correcting the most common problems in student essays.

Grammar Tips

Tips on Verbs

DON'T SWITCH VERB TENSES WITHOUT A GOOD REASON.

- x   When I *arrive* at work late, I *felt* I needed a caffeine fix. Off to the machine I *go*.
- ✔   When I *arrived* at work late, I *felt* I needed a caffeine fix. Off to the machine I *went*.

Now, all the verbs "arrived," "felt," "needed," and "went" are in the past tense.

MAKE THE VERB AGREE WITH THE SUBJECT OF THE SENTENCE.

- x   One of Joe's eyelids *were* cut.
- ✔   *One* of Joe's eyelids *was* cut.

The subject of the sentence is "one," not "eyelids." Only one was cut. Therefore the verb must be singular to agree with the singular subject "one."

x The *green* of the trees *symbolize* hope.

✔ The *green* of the trees *symbolizes* hope.

It is the green that symbolizes hope, not the trees. Therefore, the verb "signifies" is singular to agree with the singular subject "green."

x In the picture, *the woman and the man represents* Adam and Eve.

✔ In the picture, *the woman and the man represent* Adam and Eve.

Here, there are two subjects, "woman" and "man," and joining them with the word "and" makes them plural. Therefore the verb must be plural too. But note: only the word "and" makes two singular subjects plural. Other connecting words such as "in addition to," "along with," and "as well as" do not make a singular subject plural.

x *Paper*, as well as pencils, *are* stocked in the storeroom.

✔ *Paper*, as well as pencils, *is* stocked in the storeroom.

x *My brother*, along with all his classmates, *collect* money for the United Way.

✔ *My brother*, along with all his classmates, *collects* money for the United Way.

Use the active voice whenever possible.

By "active voice," we mean that the subject is the doer of the action. Verbs that are active have more life than verbs that are passive. Contrast the following two sentences.

x I *was bitten* by your budgie! (passive voice)

✔ Your budgie *bit* me! (active voice)

In the first sentence, the subject is the receiver of the action; therefore, the sentence loses its force. The second sentence puts the emphasis on the doer of the action, the bird.

The passive voice will often make your sentences sound awkward and pompous.

x At recess, *time was taken* to play games and eat cookies. (passive)

✔ At recess, the students *took* time to play games and eat cookies. (active)

x *It is to be hoped* that the patient will soon improve. (passive)

✔ *I hope* that patient will soon improve. (active)

Sometimes, however, you can use the passive voice when the doer of the action is unknown.

✔ Windows in the new hospital wing *were smashed* during the riots.

Tips on Pronouns

Pronouns refer back to nouns that precede them. These nouns are called antecedents. Every pronoun must have a clear noun antecedent. The following sentences show the correct use of pronouns.

✔ Thomas Edison is the *man who* invented the light bulb.

The pronoun "who" refers back to the noun antecedent "man."

✔ Move the *table that* is in the hall.

"That" is the pronoun referring back to the noun antecedent "table."

✔ The *bird* opened *its* beak.

In this sentence, "bird" is the noun antecedent of the pronoun "its." Notice the correct spelling of the pronoun. "It's" is a contraction for "it is."

ENSURE THAT PRONOUNS HAVE A CLEAR NOUN ANTECEDENT

   x   At many dump sites in resort areas, *they* fail to throw their garbage into the pit.

Because "they" has no noun antecedent, we're not sure who "they" are.

   ✔   At many dump sites in resort areas, *cottagers* fail to throw their garbage into the pit.

   x   People starting exercise programs often don't warm up, *which* causes their muscles to become over-strained.

In this sentence, the pronoun "which" has no clear noun antecedent. It simply refers to a whole general idea. Because the pronoun has no noun "parent" to which to attach itself, it is called an "orphan pronoun." Such a sentence must be rewritten. Often it is best to recast the sentence, eliminating "which" completely.

   ✔   Failure to warm up before exercising often causes muscle strain.

   x   Dog-trainers now consider rewards to be the most effective way of teaching canines to obey. *This* has meant a decline in the use of punishments.

In this example, the pronoun "this" is an orphan because it has no clear noun antecedent to which it belongs. "This" refers instead to the whole general idea expressed in the preceding sentence. The best way to correct the error is to wipe out the orphan pronoun completely and reword the sentence.

✔ Dog-trainers now use rewards more often than punishments for the effective teaching of canine obedience.

PRONOUNS SHOULD AGREE WITH THEIR ANTECEDENTS

x   *Everybody* must remember to do *their* share to reduce pollution. Words like "everybody," "somebody," and "someone" are singular. Therefore the pronouns that refer to them must be singular, too.

✔ *Everybody* must remember to do *his or her* share to reduce pollution.

If the "his/her" seems awkward, put everything into the plural.

✔ *All citizens* should remember to do *their* share to reduce pollution.

USE DIFFERENT FORMS OF PRONOUNS ACCORDING TO THEIR USE AS SUBJECTS OR OBJECTS

These are the personal pronouns that can be used as the subject of the sentence: I, you, he, she, it, we, you (plural), they. The following examples show you how to use pronouns as subjects.

✔ *I* gave the book to Juana.
✔ *You* wrote a good report.
✔ *He/she/it* was still missing.
✔ *We* lounged around.
✔ *You* must vote in the election.
✔ *They* always pay their Visa account promptly.

Students seldom have problems with pronoun subjects. Where they do have problems is with pronoun objects. A pronoun object comes after a verb or preposition. These are the personal pronouns that are used as objects: me, you, him, her, it, us, you (plural), them.

✔ Juana gave the book back to *me*. (me: object of the preposition "to")
✔ The dog saw *you* and charged. (you: object of the verb "saw")
✔ The noise came from behind *him/her/it*. (him/her/it: object of the preposition "behind")

- ✔ Ben Johnson beat *us* to the finish line. (us: object of the verb "beat")
- ✔ The rug under *them* was dirty. (them: object of the preposition "under")

Problems with pronoun objects occur in sentences when another word is put in front of the pronoun. While nobody would say "Juana gave the book back to I," many people say, incorrectly, "Juana gave the book back to Joe and I." Here are some more examples.

- x Daily exercises help Mother and *I* to keep fit.
- ✔ Daily exercises help Mother and *me* to keep fit.
- x The dog saw you and *I* and charged.
- ✔ The dog saw you and *me* and charged.
- x My friend gave the information to my sister and *we*.
- ✔ My friend gave the information to my sister and *us*.

Here is an easy test if you have problems with this grammatical point...

Would you say "The car came towards I"? Of course not! You would say "The car came towards me." It does not matter, then, if there is another person in front of "me." The correct pronoun is still the object, "me."

- ✔ The car came towards Hugh, Manjula, and *me* as we were going up the hill.

DON'T USE APOSTROPHES WITH THESE POSSESSIVE FORMS OF THE PRONOUNS: YOURS, HIS, HERS, ITS, OURS, THEIRS, WHOSE

The most common problem is with the possessive pronoun "its."

- x The *Sunday Times* is popular for *it's* book review section.
- ✔ The *Sunday Times* is popular for *its* book review section.

Use the word "it's" *only* when you need the contraction for "it is." Remember, too, that the form *its'* exists only as a nasty error in student papers. Wipe it from your minds. Students sometimes confuse "whose" and "who's." Remember that "who's" is used only as a contraction for "who is."

- ✔ *Whose* book is this?
- ✔ *Who's* going to the dance tonight?

Avoiding Sentence Problems

AVOID UNCLEAR REFERENCES

- x *Sitting in the car, a moose crossed the road.*

"Sitting" is a verbal which does not have an agent in the main part of the sentence; that is, we don't know *who* was sitting. Therefore the verbal attaches itself to the noun "moose" with ridiculous results.

   ✔ Sitting in the car, *we* waited for the moose to cross the road.

   x   By purchasing this product, *it* will give you the illusion of wealth.
Here the agent seems to be "it," but "it" cannot do purchasing.

   ✔ By purchasing this product, *the consumer* will have the illusion of wealth.

   x   In order to become successful, *it* depends on how hard-working you are.

   ✔ In order to become successful, *you* must be hard-working.

   x   After reading most of the play, *it* becomes obvious that the main character will die.

   ✔ After reading most of the play, *we* see clearly that the main character will die.

USE PARALLEL STRUCTURE

In each part of the sentence where there are equivalent ideas, the grammatical structure must also be equivalent. Some examples will make this point clearer.

   x   Nazia likes *swimming, skiing,* and *to golf.*
There are three equivalent ideas here; namely, the three sports which Nazia likes. Obviously the first two are in equivalent grammatical structure, but the last one is not.

   ✔ Nazia likes *swimming, skiing,* and *golfing.*

   x   These people have *no sense of loyalty* or *standing up for what they believe in.*
There are two areas in which these people are deficient, but the second is not in the same grammatical structure as the first.

   ✔ These people have *no sense of loyalty* or *of commitment.*

   x   He took the child on outings to *the zoo, swimming,* and *the Science Centre.*
There are three places to which the child went, but the second one is obviously not parallel to the others in grammatical structure.

   ✔ He took the child on outings to *the zoo, the pool,* and *the Science Centre.*

Using parallel structure is a way of giving emphasis to your sentences. Everyone who has studied Latin remembers Julius Caesar's famous statement: *"Veni, vidi, vici."* *("I came, I saw, I conquered.")* Sentences in parallel structure have a way of imprinting themselves on the mind.

Avoiding Sentence Fragments

A sentence makes a complete statement. A fragment is an incomplete piece of a sentence. Here are ways to avoid fragments.

DON'T USE VERBS ENDING IN "ING" AS MAIN VERBS

x   Improper stretching *being* the main cause of muscle pulls.
✔ Improper stretching *is* the main cause of muscle pulls.
x   The dominant colour *being* gold which symbolizes wealth and good fortune.
✔ The dominant colour *is* gold which symbolizes wealth and good fortune.
x   *The man sitting in the front row of the theatre.* (There is no main verb in this sentence.)
✔ The police arrested the man sitting in the front row of the theatre.

The main verb is now "arrested."

✔ *The man sitting in the front row of the theatre became ill.*

The main verb is now "became."

✔ The man was sitting in the front row of the theatre.

The helping verb "was" has been tacked on to "sitting," thereby making a complete main verb.

DON'T LET A PORTION OF YOUR SENTENCE SPLINTER OFF
FROM THE MAIN IDEA

x   The protagonist of the story is Jake Barnes. *A man who has suffered physical injury during the war.*
✔ The protagonist of the story is Jake Barnes, a man who has suffered physical injury during the war.

Using a comma, not a period, to separate parts of a sentence will fix this splintered fragment.

x   If the publisher decides not to pursue the publication of this project with the author. All rights shall revert to the author.

✔ If the publisher decides not to pursue the publication of this project with the author, all rights shall revert to the author.

Using Punctuation Correctly

The whole puzzling question of where to put punctuation can be simplified if you consider the advice of Canadian writer and editor, Arnold Edinborough:

> When you pause for breath it's a comma; when you stop for breath it's a full stop; and when you swallow it's a paragraph.

Edinborough's three rules are a good general guide. Reading your essay drafts aloud will give you a good sense of what he means.

When Edinborough talks about starting a new paragraph when you swallow, he's indicating that your paragraphs should not be too long. Notice that essays in magazines have fairly short paragraphs. Large unbroken blocks of print are intimidating to the eye, and keep people from reading.

For more information on pauses and stops, read on.

The Pause for Breath — The Comma

PUT COMMAS AROUND ANY PART OF THE SENTENCE THAT YOU COULD LIFT OUT OF THE SENTENCE WITHOUT CHANGING ITS BASIC MEANING

✔ Most insects love moisture. Mosquitoes, *more than any other insect*, multiply where there are stagnant ponds.

In the second sentence, "more than any other insect" is a phrase that connects the second sentence with the first. While it is important for this reason, you could remove it without altering the basic meaning of the sentence.

✔ Winston Churchill, *one of Britain's most famous leaders*, mobilized a nation for the war effort.

It is impossible to read this sentence without pausing for breath after "Winston Churchill" and after "leaders." As well, the position that Churchill held could be omitted without changing the basic information that the sentence contains about his contribution to the war. For these reasons, commas are required.

✔ The split in the Communist party was, *you might say*, the least of Gorbachev's problems.

Note that the phrase "you might say" is an interrupter to the main flow of the sentence and is therefore surrounded by commas.

INSERT A COMMA TO MARK A PAUSE AFTER INTRODUCTORY WORDS

> ✔ *Despite recent setbacks and difficulties*, native leaders will continue to seek recognition of their aboriginal rights.

Notice how the sentence deflects into its main point after the opening phrase.

> ✔ *As the leaders of the Economic Community drafted their final communique*, it became evident that they would reach no consensus.
> ✔ *Mikhail Gorbachev announced*, ''There is no way to recapture the past.''

Notice that when the sentence shifts direction after the introductory identification of the speaker, you must make a pause and insert a comma before the quotation.

The Stop for Breath — The Full Stop

Full stops are of three types: the period (the dead stop), and the semi-colon and the colon (the running stops). Here are some tips for avoiding confusion in the use of these punctuation marks.

AVOID THE COMMA SPLICE

Don't mistake a full stop for a pause. The comma splice occurs when you splice (or join) two sentences together with commas, instead of making a full stop.

> x Laura Ashley fans can buy a complete range of co-ordinated home fabrics and furniture, they can even get flowered soup tureens to match their window shades.

Reading these words aloud, you can see that there must be a full stop after the work ''furniture.''

> ✔ Laura Ashley fans can buy a complete range of co-ordinated home fabrics and furniture. They can even get flowered soup tureens to match their window shades.

There is a second way to correct the comma splice. If the sentences are closely related, the writer may wish to make a rolling stop instead of a dead stop. In this case a semi-colon is also correct.

> ✔ Laura Ashley fans can buy a complete range of co-ordinated home

fabrics and furniture; they can even get flowered soup tureens to match their window shades.

You use commas to link sentences *only* when the sentences are very short.

> ✔ It's an all too familiar story. He took heroin, he became addicted, he died.

Even worse than the comma splice is the run-on sentence, where the writer fails even to pause and runs right through one sentence into the next with no punctuation.

> x Steve Bauer is an excellent all-round cyclist however he claims that he is not as good a climber as some of the past Tour de France winners have been.

You need superhuman breath control to read that one without a stop!

> ✔ Steve Bauer is an excellent all-round cyclist. However he claims that he is not as good a climber as some of the past Tour de France winners have been.

Note that since these two sentences are closely related, a semicolon to separate them would also be correct.

> ✔ Steve Bauer is an excellent all-round cyclist; however he claims that he is not as good a climber as some of the past Tour de France winners have been.

If you insert "and" or "but" between the sentences, you may use a comma.

> ✔ Steve Bauer is an excellent all-round cyclist, but he claims that he is not as good a climber as some of the past Tour de France winners have been.

To sum up: Periods are always correct between sentences. Semicolons are correct, too, to separate sentences that are closely related in thought. Commas are used to link sentences *only* if the sentences are connected by "and" or "but" or if they are very short.

The Colon

USE THE COLON AFTER A COMPLETE SENTENCE TO MARK A STOP
FOR BREATH BEFORE A LIST

> ✔ Vancouver's Granville Island attracts a variety of tourists: photo-

graphers who want interesting pictures of the harbour, "yuppies" who itch to use their charge cards at the craft shops, and food addicts who delight in the fresh produce in the markets.

In this sentence, the phrase "a variety of tourists" signals a list and indicates a need for a stop before it.
Don't use a colon unless it follows a complete sentence.

   x   Three reasons why business firms have difficulty getting workers are: two few young people coming into the job market, too many veterans taking early retirement, and not enough skilled technicians.

   ✓   There are three reasons why business firms have difficulty getting workers: too few young people coming into the job market, too many veterans taking early retirement, and not enough skilled technicians.

   x   The shopping list included: green peppers, carrots, milk, and bread.

   ✓   The shopping list included these items: green peppers, carrots, milk and bread.

USE THE COLON AFTER A COMPLETE SENTENCE WHICH INTRODUCES
A LONG QUOTATION

   ✓   Dale Giffen says this in her prize-winning essay on the drug crisis: "Teenagers have to be able to talk to their parents about *anything*, because in today's society, anything can happen. I know for me, one of the main problems was I felt I could not approach my parents."

The Apostrophe

One other punctuation mark that gives trouble is the apostrophe. Let's review the main rules.

USE APOSTROPHES TO SHOW POSSESSION

a) To make a singular word possessive, always add 's.

   ✓   the film debut of John Bon Jovi = John Bon *Jovi's* film debut
   ✓   the sabbatical leave of Shelley Boyes = Shelley *Boyes's* sabbatical leave
   ✓   the house of my brother-in-law = my *brother-in-law's* house

b) To make a plural word possessive, add only ' when the plural word ends in s. But if the plural word does not end in s, add 's for the possessive form.

   ✓   a car from General Motors = a General *Motors'* car

- the quality of the cars = the *cars'* quality
- the tails of the mice = the *mice's* tails
- the rights of women = *women's* rights

c) Notice that when two people own the same item, only the last person's name has an apostrophe.

- John and *Mario's* bicycles (both boys share possession of the bicycles)
- *John's* and *Mario's* bicycles (each boy separately owns a number of bicycles)

NEVER USE WITH PLURAL WORDS UNLESS THERE IS POSSESSION

Compare

- *Canadians* were divided on the issue of free trade with the United States.

and

- *Canadians' opinions* on free trade were very mixed.

APOSTROPHES CAN ALSO BE USED TO SHOW CONTRACTIONS (LETTERS LEFT OUT), BUT APOSTROPHES ARE *NEVER* USED IN VERBS UNLESS THERE IS A CONTRACTION

- x   Our family *buy's* a lot at the Canadian Tire store.
- Our family *buys* a lot at the Canadian Tire store.
- Our *family's* going to the Canadian Tire store. The apostrophe here indicates the omission of the "i" in the verb "is."

PERSONAL PRONOUNS *NEVER* TAKE AN APOSTROPHE TO SHOW POSSESSION. THIS IS ONE OF THE WEIRD RULES IN THE ENGLISH LANGUAGE.

- *His* car is parked.
- *Its* feathers are ruffled.
- That house is *ours.*
- *Hers* was the only book lost.
- *Whose* health card is this?
- I took my coat to school, but they left *theirs* at home.

Getting Your Numbers Right

Here is a short summary of the rules for using numbers correctly in your essay.

Words or Numerals?

Generally, use words for all numbers from one to nine, and numerals for anything over nine.

> ✓ The patient had been hospitalized *five* times with a temperature of over *107°*.

But related numbers should be put into the same style.

> ✓ Studies show that *2* out of every *10* adolescents suffer some marked hearing loss.

Other Exceptions

A combination of words and figures is preferable in very large numbers.

> ✓ It is better to write *8.5 billion* people than *8,500,000,000* people.

If figures occur very seldom in your essay, you may put them into words as long as they require not more than two words.

> ✓ Your essay should not be longer than *two thousand* words.

Never start a sentence with a figure in numerals.

> x   *90* years ago, most women did not have the right to vote.
> ✓ *Seventy-five* people were present at the dinner.

Use figures rather than words with abbreviations or symbols:

> ✓ $2   ✓ 45%   ✓ 3 a.m. (but *three o'clock*)

Dates

a) Use either *18 December 1902* or *December 18, 1902*. Don't mix the styles.
b) Spell out centuries and use a hyphen between adjectives.

> ✓ Darwin was the most prominent influence on science in the *nineteenth* century.
> ✓ Darwin was a *nineteenth-century* scientist.

It is acceptable to express decades in figures.

> ✓ Darwin wrote his theories of evolution in the *1850s*.

Of course, there's more to good writing than just getting your grammar, spelling, punctuation, and numbers right. The following section contains tips that can help you write with flair and impact.

AVOIDING DOUBLESPEAK

"Doublespeak" is a term which describes the use of unnecessarily difficult or evasive words and phrases where simple, straightforward ones would do. Rick Coe of Simon Fraser University collects examples of doublespeak and gives a booby prize for the worst ones. You will enjoy some of the following items from his collection.

DOUBLESPEAK

— From the Ontario College of Nurses: *The Level II nurse uses probability and decision criteria in order to select the nursing diagnosis with the highest likelihood of occurrence.* Translation: Nurses should look at the patient's symptoms before deciding what to do.
— From an anecdotal report card: *The student depends on others to do his work and borrows items from the teacher without permission.* Translation: The student cheats and steals.
— A Mr. Universe title-winner admits taking *pharmaceutical training aids.* Translation: He admits taking anabolic steroids.
— From a fire department: *We found the victim in a non-viable condition.* Translation: He was dead.

Why do people use doublespeak? There are perhaps several answers. They may think that using complicated language will make what they say seem more important. More serious may be the deliberate desire to evade, obscure, or deny the truth. In your essays, always choose the simple phrase over the complicated one, and the clear sentence over the murky alternative.

AVOIDING CLICHÉS

Clichés are worn-out expressions that have been recycled so often that they have no longer have much meaning. "Have a nice day" probably means nothing more than "get lost." Poor writers and poor speakers often use clichés as a substitute for thought. You are probably all familiar with speeches at Commencement that go like this:

x   I say to you young people on whom the fate of the nation rests, go forth into a new tomorrow with your hopes high. You alone can make the world a better place. With your youth and energy you can forge a better world for us all, a world where opportunities will be equal for all and where men and women can live together in peace and harmony.

Such a speech is easy to write because it is simply a piecing together of tired phrases that everyone has heard a hundred times before. The writer George Orwell comments that such an accumulation of stale words chokes off thought like "tea leaves blocking a sink."

Here are some more examples of tired phrases.

CLICHÉS

good as gold	new and innovative
challenging opportunities	poignant memories
the free world	male chauvinist pig
get on the bandwagon	use a little elbow grease
get down to brass tacks	give it 110%
environmentally friendly	we need a level playing field
turn over a new leaf	friends are always there for you

If phrases spring onto your page easily, chances are that they are clichés. Set these ready-made phrases aside, and try to say something fresh.

AVOIDING SLANG

While it is perfectly natural and right to use slang in your conversations with your friends, remember that slang is inappropriate in formal writing.

x   Robert Bourassa *took a spaz* during the premiers' conference at Meech Lake.

Note how the slang phrase stands out like Spandex biking shorts among tuxedos.

✔ Robert Bourassa *became upset* during the premiers' conference at Meech Lake.

Slang may of course be appropriate if you are writing an informal essay or if you are reporting the exact words of someone whom you are interviewing.

✔ Country singer k.d. lang comments, "Singing is *the ultimate. It's what I live for.*"

The slang expression "the ultimate" is fine in this example because it conveys lang's enthusiasm more exactly than a more formal expression would have.

USING REPETITION TO ADD EMPHASIS

Here is an example of effective repetition from one of Churchill's most famous wartime speeches.

✔ *We shall* go on to the end, *we shall fight* in France, *we shall fight* on the seas and oceans, *we shall fight* with growing confidence and growing strength in the air, *we shall* defend our island, whatever the cost may be, *we shall fight* on the beaches, *we shall fight* on the landing grounds, *we shall fight* in the fields and in the streets, *we shall fight* in the hills: *we shall* never surrender.

Both the dramatic simplicity of the diction and the rhythm of the repeated phrase "we shall fight" caught the mood of the times and translated it into action.

In the business world, advertisers too know the value of effective repetition. The following soap ad implants in the consumer's mind the idea that its product is supposedly filled with moisturizers that "condition" your skin.

What looks best on a *conditioned* body? *Conditioned* skin.

AVOIDING REDUNDANCY

Of course, there are repetitions that are unintentional and therefore ineffective. These we call redundancy — where ideas are repeated for no good reason.

x   If we *co-operate together*, we can win.
x   Being *independent, I don't have to rely* on anyone.
x   The sun is *descending down* into the ocean.
x   This movie was the *funniest* I have *ever* seen *in my whole life.*

x   There is no doubt that Margaret Laurence made an excellent *choice* in *choosing* Dylan Thomas's poem as her epigraph.

The repetitions in the above sentences show that the writers have lost control over their craft. Redundancy is sloppy writing. Here are the corrections.

- If we co-operate, we can win.
- I don't have to rely on anyone.
- The sun is descending into the ocean.
- This movie was the funniest I have seen.
- There is no doubt that Margaret Laurence made an excellent choice in Dylan Thomas's poem as her epigraph.

USING PARALLEL AND BALANCED SENTENCES

Parallel structures can imprint themselves on the listeners' minds. One student uses parallel structure to make an appeal for the continuance of the traditional commencement ritual.

- It is a time to return to the place where you spent the last five years and a chance to bid a final farewell to the people who shared this time with you — laughed and cried with you, shaped your way of thinking and your outlook on life.

Commercials often use parallelism. An ad for jeans uses the technique to emphasize that the jeans fit the natural rhythms of a person's life.

- Dig in the garden. Wash the car. Go to a movie. Walk the dog. Burp the kid.

Balance is a special kind of parallel structure. A balanced structure proceeds in paired groupings, each item in the pair about the same length, of the same importance, and with the same grammatical structure. The following memorable examples will give you an idea of the effectiveness of balance.

- Ask not what your country can do for you — ask what you can do for your country. — from the inaugural address of John F. Kennedy.
- It was the best of times, it was the worst of times . . . it was the spring of hope, it was the winter of despair. — from the opening paragraph of Dickens's *Tale of Two Cities*.

USING COMPARISONS TO GIVE FLAIR TO YOUR WRITING

We use comparisons all the time in our ordinary speech to give colour and clarity to our ideas. Unfortunately some of these comparisons have been used so often that they have lost their originality and become clichés. We talk about extending the *horizons* of science, analyzing the *climate* of public opinion, *turning over a new leaf*, keeping the *political machine well oiled* with donations, and acting *like a bull in a china shop*.

But fresh comparisons can be an effective way to help readers understand the concepts you are presenting in your essay. One student, analyzing the parent-child relationship, wrote: *"Parents are like blankets. They can give you warmth, but they can also smother you."*

Another young writer described divorce as being *"like a scalpel severing infected flesh from a body."* Comparisons like these help to make abstract ideas specific and concrete.

6

ADDING THE FINISHING TOUCHES

Presenting the Essay

However profound your thoughts, however brilliant your prose, however well-documented your opinions, you will make a poor impression and perhaps face a lower mark if your essay is not properly typed or keyboarded. A messy paper is difficult to read. And a frustrated reader of your paper is not likely to give full attention to your ideas or award you a top mark. So why not put yourself in the best possible position by submitting an impressive-looking piece of work? Even if you have to get someone else to type your essay or use a computer at your school, the effort will be worthwhile.

In order to make sure that the typed paper is appealing to the eye, you should follow certain standardized guidelines.

Paper

Type on standard 216 mm × 280 mm (8½ × 11 inch) blank white paper, like that used for photocopies. Non-standard sizes of paper, coloured paper, or lined paper are unacceptable and make your work look unprofessional. And, by the way, type on only one side of the sheet. Teachers often like to lay all the pages of your essay out in front of them. They can't do that if you've typed on the back of the sheets.

Margins

In order to frame your essay properly, you should leave generous margins on the top, bottom, and sides of each page. A general rule is to leave 25 mm (one inch) on each side and 25 mm (one inch) at top and bottom.

Spacing

Essays submitted to a teacher or an editor are always double-spaced. Double-spacing makes the text more readable and eases corrections by both author and marker.

Title Page

Like the cover of a book, a title page gives the reader important information about writer and subject, and acts as a sort of protective jacket for your work.

Making a title page is easy and takes only a couple of minutes. You should centre the title just a little bit above the middle of the page. Below the title, about two-thirds of the way down the page, type your name, your teacher's name, the course name, and the date. These items should be positioned two-thirds of the way across the page, one above the other. (Please refer to the research essay in the Appendix for a sample title page.)

If, however, your teacher does not like title pages, then all of the above information can go on the first page of your essay. Your name, teacher's name, course name, and date can be typed at the left margin and double-spaced. Below this, you should centre the title, again being careful not to underline. A sample of this alternative appears at the top of the report found in the Appendix. It's also acceptable to use the alternate format on an essay.

Page Numbering

Numbering your pages will prevent confusion if the pages are misplaced. Numbering starts with the first page of text, which means that the title page DOES NOT count as page one. Further, you can omit putting the number "1" on page one, beginning with page 2. Usually the page number is placed one-half inch below the top edge of the page, so that it is well set off from the text. If you fear that parts of your essay might get lost, it's also a good idea to put your surname at the top of each page, just to the left of the page number.

Tables and Illustrations

Tables and illustrations can be effective in presenting easy-to-read or important explanatory information. In general, tables contain rows and columns of data. Illustrations (called "figures") are pictures, drawing, or sketches. Normally, it's best to put tables and illustrations within the body of your essay or report, rather than hiding them away in some easily-ignored appendix.

You should make reference within the body of your essay to the tables and figures you include. Here are some examples of how to mention them within the text.

While many of us think of radioactive elements as being toxic for centuries, some substances, such as those used in medical tests, have half-lives of only minutes or hours (Table 1).

The fiery phoenix (Fig. 3) is an important mythological symbol of rebirth.

Place tables and illustrations as close as possible to the part of the text that they explain. It's important to label them with descriptive headings such as "Table 1: Half-Lives of Various Radioactive Substances" or "Figure 3: Phoenix." The report in the Appendix shows how to label. In both cases, you must also show, at the bottom of the table or figure, where the information came from, if it is not your own work. To credit the source, use the same format as for a footnote, but without numbering it as a footnote. The following example shows you what a table looks like and how its source is cited.

Table 1: Canada's International Trade, 1981-1991:
(millions of 1986 dollars)

Year	Exports	Imports	Trade Balance
1981	101,853	105,313	− 3,460
1982	99,637	89,343	10,294
1983	106,017	97,395	8,622
1984	124,785	114,058	10,727
1985	132,218	123,935	8,283
1986	138,119	133,369	4,750
1987	142,942	142,678	264
1988	156,528	162,385	− 5,857
1989	157,952	172,729	− 14,777
1990	164,507	176,010	− 11,503
1991	165,326	179,952	− 14,626

Source: <u>Bank of Canada Review</u> October 1992: H3.

Binding or Covering Your Work

Many teachers dislike any type of binder or cover for an essay, as they make it much harder to write comments. They also prevent a side-by-side examination of different sections of the essay.

Other teachers believe that packaging an essay is a necessary finishing touch. However, even if you bind your essay, don't enclose each page in a plastic sheath if your instructors want to be able to write comments. Remember that no one ever caught a fatal disease from an unprotected piece of paper!

Overall, it's best to ask your instructors what they prefer: a folder, a paperclip, or even a simple staple.

Documenting Your Information Sources

Before you put your essay into final form, you must be certain that you have properly documented the sources you have used. Acknowledging information sources accomplishes several important purposes. It indicates to your teachers what are and aren't your ideas; it allows them to analyze the source of certain opinions, statistics, and observations; and it gives due credit to others for the use of their material. But the most important purpose of documentation is to avoid charges of plagiarism.

Plagiarism

Plagiarism (from the Latin "plagiarius," meaning kidnapper) is a serious academic offence that many students commit unknowingly. Put simply, plagiarism is the use of other people's words, work, or ideas without proper acknowledgment. Plagiarism can take many forms. It can involve copying passages word-for-word without stating the source of the quotation. But you are also plagiarizing if you put other people's opinions in your own words without crediting the original source. Many students simply do not realize that this second form of plagiarism is just as serious as the first. Finally, plagiarism includes submitting an essay written by someone else.

For example, in doing research for an essay about America's role in world affairs, you may read about Paul Kennedy's theory that for several decades U.S. power has been in relative decline because of something called "imperial overstretch." In your essay, you cannot rephrase his theory by stating that the U.S.

has lost power because of its excessive global military and diplomatic commitments unless you acknowledge that the idea really belongs to Professor Kennedy. By admitting that you did not come up with the concept yourself, you avoid committing a serious academic offence.

What to Document

As well as giving credit for others' opinions, you should also document the source of important facts that will not be known to the average reader. While there may be no need to show how you knew that Ronald Reagan served two terms as U.S. President or that the chemical formula for water is H_2O, you should certainly tell where you learned that Canada had a current account deficit in 1987.

In summary, you must document the opinions or words of others, as well as the origin of facts and statistics that are not well known. The sources you cite can vary from books and magazines to films, videotapes, televisions programs, and even interviews.

How to Document

THE NEW EASY METHOD

Documentation of sources isn't really all that hard, especially since the Modern Language Association of America has come up with a simplified method. (See the research essay in the Appendix as an example of how the new method is used.) All you have to do is put the author's last name and the page number in parentheses after the statement you wish to document. The reader can then look at the "Works Cited" at the end of the essay in order to get more information about the book, such as the publisher's name. Footnotes or endnotes are no longer necessary.

For example, a reference to Charles Dickens's *A Tale of Two Cities* would appear like this in an essay:

> Most central to his point of view is that it was really "the worst of times" (Dickens 3).

If, however, you mention the author's name within the text, you need only give the page number. In this case, the above example would read:

Most central to Dickens's point of view is that it was really "the worst of times" (3).

When you list more than one book by the same author, it is important to identify the title as well as the author and the page number. The title of the book can be abbreviated but still must be recognizable. If, for example, you were writing an essay about several books by Charles Dickens, you could refer to *A Tale of Two Cities* as *Tale* and to *Nicholas Nickleby* as *Nickleby*.

THE TRADITIONAL METHOD

If your teacher does not accept the new, simple style, you will have to use the old, yet universally recognized, procedure for footnotes and endnotes.

Footnotes are numbered references to your sources which are placed at the bottom of each page of text and separated from the text by a short horizontal line. Endnotes, as the name suggests, are put at the end of your essay text rather than at the foot of each page. Footnotes and endnotes are usually numbered in ascending order throughout the entire text, with the number being placed slightly above the line, as in the following example:

> As a young man, Winston Churchill realized that "as long as the interests of two nations coincide . . . they will be allies."[1]

As you can see, the superscripted footnote or endnote number comes at the end of the sentence in which the quotation (or reference to someone else's work) occurs.

Footnotes for books have the following characteristics:

- the footnotes at the bottom of each page are separated from the rest of the text by a straight, two-inch line just below the main text;
- the first line is indented five spaces, but subsequent lines begin at the margin;
- the footnote number comes first and is raised slightly above the line;
- next comes the author's name (first name and then last) followed by a comma, and then the title of the book, which is underlined;
- then you find the publication information which is put in parentheses and looks this way (place of publication: publisher, date);

- finally, you include the page number(s) and a period to end the footnote.

For example, the above quotation from Winston Churchill would have this accompanying footnote at the bottom of the page where the sentence appeared:

[1]David Reynolds, The Creation of the Anglo-American Alliance, 1937-41: A Study in Competitive Cooperation (Chapel Hill, NC: University of North Carolina Press, 1981) vi.

Since this procedure may still be a bit hard to understand at first, it's best to look at some more actual examples of footnotes which are given below.

Books

[1] Thomas Hobbes, Leviathan (London: Penguin, 1985) 421.

[2] Joseph Gibaldi and Walter S. Achtert, eds., MLA Handbook for Writers of Research Papers, 3rd ed. (New York: MLA, 1988) 94-95.

Magazines

[3] Ian McGuigan, "Debt Service with a Smile," Moneywise March 1989: 52.

[4] Bryan Hodgson, "Antarctica: A Land of Isolation No More," National Geographic April 1990: 22-23.

Newspapers

[5] Robert Bothwell, "Canadian whines dissolve a nation," Globe and Mail 28 May 1990: A7.

[6] Lisa Belkin, "Bored With the Usual Fireworks? Try This," New York Times 28 May 1990, late ed.: 1, 8.

Interviews

[7] Janet Wilson, personal interview, 23 Feb. 1990.

[8] Barbara Johnson, interview, As It Happens, CBC Radio, CBL, Toronto, 25 Sept. 1990.

Television and Radio Programs

[9] The Kids in the Hall, exec. prod. Lorne Michaels, CBC, CBLT, Toronto, 29 Jan. 1990.

Films, Videotapes, Filmstrips, and Slide Shows

[10] Circulation: The Flow of Blood, motion picture loop, Encyclopaedia Britannica, 1963 (one colour super 8 mm cartridge).

[11] Learning Through Rewards, sound filmstrip, by B.F. Skinner, Multi-Media Productions, Inc., 1974 (one cassette, one filmstrip, one teacher's manual).

Recordings

[12] Maurice Ravel, Piano Concerto in G major, The World of Ravel, cond. Istvan Kertesz, London Symphony Orchestra, Polygram, SPA4069, 1975.

Subsequent References

Although you must use a full citation the first time that you make a footnote reference to a source, for subsequent references you can use an abbreviated form of footnote. In general, you only have to mention the author's last name and the page number. Thus, a later footnote reference to David Reynold's book (this time to page 87) may appear as:

[13] Reynolds 87.

If you are using more than one book by the same author, then you should also include a shortened version of the title after the author's name. For example, later references to Dickens's *Tale of Two Cities* and *Nicholas Nickleby* may appear as:

[14] Dickens, *Tale* 304.

[15] Dickens, *Nickleby* 127.

Using Quotations

One of the things that separates a beginning writer from an expert is the ability to work quotations smoothly into the essay or report. The effective use of another person's words can help to strengthen your argument and give that "touch of class" to your prose. Remember, however, that your essay should never be just a string of quotations connected by a few sentences of your own. Use a quotation only when it makes an interesting hook or backs up an important point that you have made.

As far as possible, try to work the quotation in so that there is no noticeable division between your wording and the author's. The following examples point out the difference between a weak use of a quotation and an effective one:

> WEAK: Albert Einstein said: "Imagination is more important than knowledge."

You will notice that there is a definite division between the student's words and those of Einstein. This is the "brute force" method of using a quotation.

> EFFECTIVE: Albert Einstein put this idea in another way when he said "imagination is more important than knowledge."

In this example, there is a smooth link between the student's words and the quotation.

> WEAK: Ms. Singh's characterization of Hamlet is as follows: "Hamlet is an extremely troubled figure." Her characterization suggests that ....
> EFFECTIVE: Ms. Singh's characterization of Hamlet as "an extremely troubled figure" suggests that...

Occasionally, you may have to make slight changes within the quotation in order to fit it smoothly with your own words. Usually these changes occur when the verb tense of a quotation is different from the verb tense in your essay or when a pronoun needs altering to fit the grammatical context of your introductory statement. Whenever you have to make these changes within a quotation, you show them by enclosing the changed words in square brackets. Again, some examples will illustrate these points.

WEAK: Erin Woodley said in her prize-winning essay that "each book we read was a new and exciting adventure."

The words in quotation marks are the original quotation. But notice that the pronoun "we" doesn't agree with the pronoun "her" in the introduction.

EFFECTIVE: Erin Woodley said in her prize-winning essay that "each book [she] read was a new and exciting adventure." OR Erin Woodley said in her prize-winning essay that "each book [her class] read was a new and exciting adventure."

The words in square brackets indicate that those words were changed to fit better into the whole sentence.

Longer Quotations

Avoid using long quotations that fill up most of a page. If you have to explain someone else's ideas, it's often better to express them in your own words rather than put down a long rambling quotation which will bore your readers and distract them from the main points of your essay. If it is absolutely necessary to use a quotation that is more than four lines long, then you have to indent the whole passage ten spaces from the left margin, while leaving out the standard quotation marks. (If the passage is indented, the reader knows automatically that it is a quotation.) Like the rest of the text, these indented excerpts are double-spaced. The following example demonstrates how one could use a longer quotation.

One of the funnier moments of Eliza Clark's <u>Miss You Like Crazy</u> occurs when the protagonist arrives at the Elvis Presley mansion in Nashville:

Before boarding the white shuttle van, Maylou checked out Elvis Stuff. She couldn't resist purchasing an Elvis cookie jar, with a head that lifted off the

body. On afterthought, she wished she'd bought the
jar post-tour, since they were out of tissue paper and
the head rattled like crazy with her every step (158).

Quotations from Poetry

Quoting from poetry requires slightly more care than quoting
from prose. First, you must remember that much of the author's
effect comes from the careful arrangement of lines. When quoting two lines of poetry, therefore, it is vital to show where the
second line begins and ends by using a slash (/) to separate the
lines. Copy carefully each punctuation mark and capital letter.
Notice that you place more than two lines of poetry in their regular lines (indented ten spaces from the margin) instead of using
slashes. Finally, quotations from poetic plays (like those by
Shakespeare) must be documented by putting the act, scene, and
line numbers in parentheses at the end of the quotation. For other
poetry, cite the line numbers of the quoted part. Here are a few
examples of how you should present poetry quotations.

Quotation from a Shakespearean play:

The "fair is foul" theme of Macbeth continues in the second
scene of the play when the injured captain complains that
from "whence comfort seem'd to come,/Discomfort swells."
(1.2.27-28)

Poetic Quotation:

John Keats' "Ode on a Grecian Urn" follows the general form
of the ode because it starts off with a direct address:

    Thou still unravished bride of quietness,

      Thou foster-child of silence and slow time,

    Sylvan historian, who canst thus express

      A flowery tale more sweetly than our rhyme: (1-4)

List of Works Cited

The list of works cited, also known as the bibliography, is the list of sources that you used while writing your research essay. The list serves several important functions: it allows readers to match up the footnote or parenthetical references with the full citation, to assess how credible and appropriate your sources are, and to find the works if they are interested in learning more about the topic. As with every other type of documentation, the list of works cited must be carefully compiled and presented in a standard, logical format. Here is the format developed by the Modern Language Association of America.

Set-up

The list of works cited appears at the very end of your research paper and starts at the top of a new page. Under the heading of "Works Cited" centred at the top of the page, you list all of the sources used (including books, magazines, newspapers, and *all* other research material). The entries are arranged in alphabetic order by the last name of the author or, if there is no known author, by the title of the work (ignoring any "a," "an," or "the" at the beginning of the title). Each entry starts with the first line at the margin, although subsequent lines are each indented five spaces, or 13 mm (half an inch). The list is double-spaced both within each entry and between the entries.

Books

Standard Entries

A standard entry for a book contains the author's last name and first name (followed by a period), the title (underlined or italicized and followed by a period), the place of publication (followed by a colon), the publisher (followed by a comma), and the date of publication (and then a period). Since this format can best be understood by seeing examples, here is a simple bibliography composed of a few books.

Works Cited

Elgin, Suzette Haden. The Last Word on the Gentle Art of Verbal Self-Defense. New York: Prentice Hall, 1987.

Kelly, Susan Baake. Mastering Wordperfect 5. Alameda, CA: Sybex, 1988.

Stockman, David A. The Triumph of Politics. New York: Avon Books, 1986.

It all seems so straightforward, doesn't it? But wait a minute. There are some times when things get tricky, such as when there are several authors per book, different editions, articles from an anthology or translations from a foreign language, to name just a few.

Two or More Authors

Bothwell, Robert, Ian Drummond, and John English. Canada, 1900-1945. Toronto: University of Toronto Press, 1987.

Kenwood, A. G. and A. L. Lougheed. The Growth of the International Economy 1820-1980. London: George Allen & Unwin, 1983.

If there are more than three authors, all you need to do is list the first author, and then type ''et al'' which is Latin for ''and others.''

Cross, T. P. et al. English Writers. Rev. ed. Boston: Ginn and Company, 1955.

Books With Editors or Compilers

Ferrell, Robert H., ed. The Twentieth Century: An Almanac.
New York: World Almanac Publications, 1985.

Landy, Alice S. and Dave Martin, comp. and ed. The Heath
Introduction to Literature. Lexington, MA: D.C. Heath, 1980.

Books With Several Editions

Elkins, Stanley M. Slavery: A Problem in American Institutional
and Intellectual Life. 3rd ed. Chicago: University of Chicago
Press, 1976.

Books Translated from a Foreign Language

Alighieri, Dante. The Purgatorio. Trans. John Ciardi. Scarborough,
ON: Mentor, 1961.

Other Sources

Dictionaries and Encyclopedias

Crane, David. "Canada-U.S. Automotive Products Agreement." The Canadian Encyclopedia. Ed. James Marsh.
2nd ed. 4 vols. Edmonton: Hurtig Publishers, 1988.

"Gibberish." The University English Dictionary. Ed. R.F.
Patterson. 1 vol. London: Number One Publishing Co.,
1974.

"Knifefishes and featherbacks." Larousse Encyclopedia of
Animal Life. Ed. Leon Bertin et al. Toronto: Hamlyn, 1971.

Poems

Milton, John. "At a Solemn Music." The English Poems of

John Milton. Ed. H.C. Beeching. Toronto: Oxford
University Press, 1951. 15-16.

Souster, Raymond. "Lake of Bays." Fifteen Winds. Ed. A.W.
Purdy. Toronto: McGraw-Hill Ryerson, 1969. 103.

Articles in an Anthology

Horowitz, G. "Conservatism, Liberalism and Socialism in
Canada: An Interpretation." Party Politics in Canada.
Ed. Hugh G. Thorburn. 5th ed. Toronto: Prentice-Hall,
1985. 41-59.

Magazine Articles

Chisholm, Patricia. "Verdict on the past: A war-crimes trial
ends with an acquittal." Maclean's 4 Jun. 1990: 58.

Maynard, Rona. "The New Executive Father." Report on
Business Magazine March 1989: 44-51.

Newspaper Articles

Ansberry, Claire. "Nannies and Mothers Struggle Over Roles
In Raising Children." Wall Street Journal 21 May 1993:
A1, A6.

Harper, Tim. "Clean air act flawed, MPs told." Toronto Star
14 Jun. 1989, late ed.: A20.

Taylor, Paul. "Doctors becoming more willing to let termi-
nally ill die in peace." Globe and Mail 19 Jun. 1990: A1,
A10.

Articles Without Authors

"Israel, in Shift, Backs 'Free' Industrial Zone." New York
Times 12 Jan. 1993: A5.

"A Who's Who of Summit's Key Players." The Houston Post 1 July 1990: J3.

Films

Jesus of Montreal. Dir. Denys Arcand. With Lothaire Bluteau, Catherine Wilkening, Johanne-Marie Tremblay, and Yves Jacques. Telefilm Canada, 1989.

Television and Radio Programs

"Goodbye, Farewell, and Amen." Prod. Thad Mumford and Dan Wilcox. Dir. Alan Alda. M*A*S*H. Exec. prod. Burt Metcalfe. CBC. CBLT, Toronto. 28 Feb. 1983.

"Why Men Act That Way." Narr. John Stossel. Writ. Steve Brand and John Stossel. 20/20. ABC. WKBW, Buffalo. 21 May 1993.

Filmstrips, Slide Shows, and Videotapes

From Newton to Modern Chromatics. Filmstrip. By Donald Pavey. Educational Productions, 1969. 37 colour frames.

The Kid Who Couldn't Miss. Videocassette. Dir. Paul Cowan. National Film Board, 1982.

What is a Painting? Slide program. The Centre for Humanities, Inc., 1982. 80 slides, one cassette tape, one record and one booklet.

Recordings

Copland, Aaron. "Appalachian Spring." Copland's Greatest Hits. Audiotape. Cond. Leonard Bernstein. New York Philharmonic. CBS Masterworks, XMT 7521, n.d.

(The n.d. means that no date was listed on the recording.)

Live Performances

Berkeley Square. By John L. Balderston. Dir. Neil Munro. Festival Theatre, Niagara-on-the-Lake, Ontario. 28 Sept. 1989.

The Day Room. By Don DeLillo. Dir. Neel Keller. Remains Theatre, Chicago, IL. 13 Jun. 1993.

Reviews

Dafoe, Chris. "Bridging the generations." Rev. of Thirteen, Hands by Carol Shields. Prairie Theatre Exchange. Globe and Mail 6 Feb. 1993: C11.

McCarthy, Michael. "The Real Story of 'the Real Thing'." Rev. of For God, Country and Coca-Cola, by Mark Pendergrast. Wall Street Journal 21 May 1993: A10.

Patterson, Alex. "A great tragedy restored." Rev. of Othello, dir. Orson Welles. Eye Weekly 4 Feb. 1993: 27.

Letters

Thurber, James. "To Herman and Dorothy Miller." 14 July 1948. In Selected Letters of James Thurber. Ed. Helen Thurber and Edward Weeks. Toronto: Little, Brown, and Co., 1981. 47.

Wilson, Michael H. Letter to the author. 22 Sept. 1984.

Interviews

Goldberg, Leonard. Personal interview. 15 April 1987.

Haney, Margaret. Telephone interview. 7 December 1990.

Kirton, John. Interview. <u>The World at Six</u>. CBC Radio. CBL, Toronto. 13 Aug. 1990.

Computer Software

Sampaleanu, Colin. <u>Telix</u>. Vers. 3.11. Computer software. Exis Inc., 1988.

Maps

<u>The Official Road Map of Ontario</u>. Map. Toronto: Ministry of Transportation and Communications, 1990.

The above examples of how to list sources in the "Works Cited" will be adequate to guide you in most situations. If after reading this chapter you are unable to figure out how to cite a source correctly, you can refer to the *MLA Handbook for Writers of Research Papers*, 3rd ed., by Joseph Gibaldi and Walter S. Achtert (New York: Modern Language Association of America, 1988).

The MLA format (used in the examples in this book) is widely accepted in many subject areas at both the high school and university level. Nevertheless, it may be necessary to learn a different citation method for a field such as law or medicine. Your instructor can inform you about other manuals to use.

APPENDIX

By showing you a research essay, an examination essay, and two related essay forms (a review and a report), this appendix gives further reinforcement for the material described in the book. All these examples were written by students.

The Research Essay

AUDIENCE

- usually your teacher, sometimes your classmates.

PURPOSE

- to demonstrate what you have learned from a variety of sources;
- to demonstrate that you have developed your own perspective on the subject as a result of your research;
- to show that you have developed your research skills;
- to prove that you know how to document your sources correctly.

LANGUAGE

- formal. There should be no contractions (like "doesn't" for "does not"), little or no use of "I" or "me," and no slang (like "slacked off" in place of "rested").

COMMENT

The following essay displays all of the criteria listed above. It also shows you how to document your sources using the new, simple method that eliminates the need for footnotes or endnotes. As well, it illustrates how to set up a cover page.

PAY ANY PRICE?:

John F. Kennedy and Civil Rights

John Birch
History 201
Ms. Smith
March 1, 1993

Birch 1

In his inaugural speech in January 1961, John F. Kennedy announced to all of the world that the United States would "pay any price, bear any burden, meet any hardship...to assure the survival and success of liberty" ("Text"). Although this lofty statement was directed primarily at America's friends and foes abroad, many hoped that it was also a promise of vigorous action in domestic policy, particularly in the field of civil rights. Kennedy's term in office showed that he was determined to see that some steps were taken to give Americans of all races the liberties granted to them under the Constitution. Through the decisive use of executive power, this President reformed many areas of federal control by implementing fair employment practices in the military and federal government, securing the desegregation of interstate bus and railway terminals, working to remove poll taxes and encourage black voter registration, and forcing universities to open their doors to blacks. While his program was certainly not a "New Frontier" in civil rights, it was clearly shrewd politically.

Housing and Home Finance Agency and even the White House. Further, for the first time, there was black representation on federal regulatory boards and in African ambassadorial positions. But while this gesture was meant to satisfy civil rights activists, it also pacified stubborn Southern whites because most of the black appointees were from the North (Harvey 24). Moreover, any future lack of action on civil rights could later be blamed on the indifference of high-ranking blacks in government instead of on the President himself. As always, Kennedy was the astute politician.

Another symbolic gesture with high political value was the forced desegregation of all interstate bus and railway facilities. Although most operators complied with the Interstate Commerce Commission's desegregation order, the Justice Department was swift to seek injunctions against those who resisted. Significantly, the Kennedy administration also concluded an agreement with Southern railroads for the integration of their terminals and then used its influence to apply similar reforms to

The first example of Kennedy's blend of pragmatism and personal belief was his move to create more racial fairness within the military. In particular, he made wide-sweeping reforms which encouraged the promotion of blacks to higher ranks and integrated all units. To oversee this project, the President appointed a Committee on Equal Opportunity which was also charged with ensuring that servicemen's families were treated fairly both on and off base. After the committee issued its report in 1963, Secretary of State Robert McNamara (under the President's specific instructions) ordered military commanders to take an active role in ensuring the complete integration of facilities (Harvey 34). Kennedy's leadership on this matter was very astute; it was an important sign that the federal government was willing to fix its own situations of inequality.

The President also tried to take a stand within the various executive agencies, especially by appointing blacks to prominent positions in the Labour Department, the Department of Health, Education and Welfare, the airports. While some may argue that Kennedy was forced to intervene after the publicity given to the 1961 freedom rides, no one can deny that his reform had a huge propaganda value and satisfied one central objective of the civil rights activists (Bickel 147). Further, these reforms were clearly in an area of federal jurisdiction, and therefore local governments had little reason to complain. The President had expertly handled another issue.

The President's pragmatic sense and expert stewardship also shone through over the question of black voting rights. Existing policies were ineffective. Although the Justice Department was empowered by existing legislation to sue for voting rights, such cases usually consumed too much time and had to be launched in many different jurisdictions. What was needed, the activists claimed, was an overall prohibition on poll taxes, literacy tests, character judgments and other barriers to equal access. Kennedy realized that to do all of this would certainly create instability among Southern

whites, so he obtained Congressional approval for a lesser ban on all poll taxes in federal elections and primaries.

The President also used executive action to encourage other electoral reforms, the most crucial of which was a voter registration campaign. In March 1962, the Voter Education Project began to send out workers (mainly to the Deep South) to encourage blacks to enumerate themselves. Although these moves did not completely satisfy civil rights activists and were by no means unqualified successes, they showed that Washington was determined to bring more equality into the democratic process.

The one thing in which the President firmly believed was the need to enforce federal court rulings. In fact, he insisted at the beginning of 1956 that regardless of the political consequences, a "Supreme Court decision is the law of the land" and must be obeyed (Schlesinger 926). He therefore took many symbolic steps to enforce the desegregation decreed in the landmark case of Brown v.

Board of Education. The first of these was the public
recognition of the justness of this decision, something
that President Eisenhower had never done (Harvey 3). He
also used fiscal power to withhold grant money (under
the National Defense Education Act among others) from
colleges that excluded blacks while simultaneously
advising school officials on how to desegregate their
facilities (Harvey 40). Admittedly, this approach was
very conservative and had very little coercive power on-
reluctant state and local governments. If Kennedy had
really wanted to force the issue, he could have withheld
all federal money (Sorenson 488). Clearly, he did not
want to risk losing all Southern support by taking such
a drastic step. Thus, the token action of cutting off a
small proportion of the funds was enough to pacify the
less militant civil rights activists while preventing a
white backlash that may have prevented his re-election.

    The President did, however, have to resort to force on
several occasions. One of these was to uphold the rights
of James Meredith, a qualified black student who was

prevented from enroling in the all-white University of
Mississippi. Although the federal courts had ordered his
acceptance by the institution, the state governor, Ross
Barnett, refused to comply. Kennedy tried repeatedly to
convince Barnett to let Meredith in, but the governor
knew that it would be politically suicidal to do so. The
President even agreed to sneak the student in through
the back door and thereby let everyone save face. But
when this proposal caved in, Kennedy realized that he
had to act forcefully.

    He dispatched federal marshals and the Mississippi
National Guard to escort Meredith into the university
(Buckley 35). On arrival, these forces were confronted by
what a witness described as "an armed and unruly
mob" (Johnson). In the ensuing skirmish, two men were
killed and over one hundred soldiers were injured. After
this shocking incident, Kennedy realized that the United
States was a long way from peacefully granting blacks
the rights and opportunities to which they were entitled.

    It is clear that even though President Kennedy was

morally committed to freeing blacks from oppression, he did not entirely succeed. Regardless of how many times he quoted Mr. Justice Harlan's statement that the "Constitution is colour-blind" (Kennedy 172), he knew very well that not all of the United States was not ready for complete racial equality. Until then, the chief executive could only try his best to bring about moderate reforms. And in doing so, he solidified his own political position with blacks and other members of the liberal movement.

WORKS CITED

Bickel, Alexander M. "Civil Rights: A New Era Opens." John F. Kennedy and the New Frontier. Ed. Aida DiPace Donald. New York: Hill and Wang, 1966. 138-164.

Buckley, Thomas. "Meredith Says He Fails to Aid Mississippi Negroes." New York Times 4 Dec. 1962: 35.

Harvey, James C. Civil Rights During the Kennedy Administration. Hattiesburg: University and College Press of Mississippi, 1971.

Johnson, Mabel. Telephone interview. 11 Apr. 1991.

Kennedy, John F. The Burden and the Glory. New York: Harper and Row, 1964.

Schlesinger, Arthur M. Jr. A Thousand Days: John F. Kennedy in the White House. Boston: Houghton Mifflin, 1965.

Sorenson, Theodore C. Kennedy. New York: Harper and Row, 1965.

"Text of Kennedy's Inaugural Outlining Policies on World Peace and Freedom." New York Times 21 Jan. 1961: 8.

The Examination Essay

- your teacher. While he or she will want to know that you have a grasp of the essentials, you will also need to show that you have thought about the facts. Therefore, as you study, develop some theories about the material you are learning. Don't just memorize.

PURPOSE

- will depend on the wording of the question. Here are a few examples of common exam directions.

---

compare: give similarities and/or differences.

contrast: give differences.

discuss: has many meanings. Ask your teacher before the examination what the word means for him or her.

explain:: assume the role of a teacher and go into enough details to make the issue clear.

illustrate:: give examples to prove a particular point.

assess:: now a favourite among English and history teachers, it means that you may prove or disprove the statement given. Example: "Assess the extent to which the French Revolution was caused by economic discontent." To answer this question, you might say that economic discontent was only one of two main factors, the other being social discontent which you would then describe in equal detail.

LANGUAGE

- formal rather than informal, but not fancy. You won't have time for a brilliant writing style.

COMMENT

This essay answers the following examination question: "Napoleon's domestic policy combined a conservative view of the social order with many of the liberal ideas of the philosophers. Illustrate this combination of conservatism and liberalism in Napoleon's domestic policy."

Napoleon's Domestic Policy: A Combination of Conservatism and Liberalism

by Phillipe Borel

At the end of the eighteenth century Napoleon Bonaparte brought to France stability and order. But his philosophy was an intricate blend of revolutionary themes and conservative beliefs.

The conservatism of Napoleon's rule is shown in many examples. The first is his agreement with the Pope to strengthen the Roman Catholic church in France. The Concordat (1801) established Catholicism as the religion of the majority and gave France a structured religious institution. Napoleon also looked to the past, as illustrated in his borrowings from the Roman way of life. In his Napoleonic Code, he incorporated many of the old Roman laws and made the father of the family powerful. He saw himself as a Caesar, unifying France. And of course, when he became Emperor in 1803, Napoleon started to establish the Imperial Guard, the Legion of Honour, and an imperial court. All of these were similar to the structure under the Bourbon Dynasty. Lastly, political structures were conservative. He was the supreme ruler, even as First Consul. Like Louis XVI he was responsible to no one, and he ruled the country directly. For additional strength, he also put his brothers on the thrones of other nations (for example, Joseph in the Kingdom of Italy), and he married Marie-Thérèse to give his own reign legitimacy in France. By these conservative measures Napoleon brought France back to a state of stability.

And yet, Napoleon also kept the liberal ideas of the Revolution and institutionalized them. Although there was no democracy, he created the illusion of one by having a Senate, a Council of State and a Tribunate. He frequently used plebiscites to approve the constitution, his "consul for life" and his role of "hereditary emperor." His constitution adopted wholly the Declaration of the Rights of Man and the Citizen and was approved overwhelmingly. His Napoleonic Code abolished all remnants of feudalism and embodied the egalitarian principles of the Revolution. Economically, he reformed the taxes so that everyone paid them. He also made the tax

system less complicated and more efficient. By 1813
France had no debt. He standardized coinage,
establishing the Bank of France in February 1800. And
he encouraged French industry by establishing tariffs.
Lastly, his administration worked practically as well as
symbolically, unlike any other. He centralized power to
unify France and to encourage nationalist emotion. He
worked tirelessly to communicate with all regions of his
country. He took power away from nobles and brought it
to Paris. In many ways, his administration resembled
more that of a republic than that of the Bourbon
monarchy.

Under Napoleon, France gained peace (at least
temporarily) and stability. Later it would come to domi-
nate Europe and change its political landscape forever.
All can be traced to the philosophy of its leader,
Napoleon, who blended conservatism and liberalism to
achieve his goals.

The Review

- people who are interested in a book, an author, a play, or a television program.

PURPOSE

- to entertain, to evaluate, and to inform.

LANGUAGE

- usually informal rather than formal; sometimes even conversational.

COMMENT

This lively review of a popular television program won second prize in a national contest sponsored by *Maclean's* magazine. Notice how the writer uses examples from the show to support his opinion. Notice, too, that the language style is less formal than that of academic papers.

Married...With Children: Fighting for

the Common Family

by Lawrence Chan

It's hip. It's hilarious. It's a hell-raiser. It's Fox's Married ... With Children. Teamed with outrageous scripts a hungry and talented staff, and a network banking their financial hopes on the show, MWC has emerged as the moral boundary-busting situation comedy hit of television.

Take one financially depressed family of four trapped in the equally disheartening suburbs of Chicago, Illinois and shake vigorously. The result is the Bundy clan. Al (Ed O'Neill) is the empty-headed husband and lifelong ladies' foot apparel account representative. A normal working stiff, he continually appears unkempt and irritated and glibly shovels insulting words to family and outsiders alike. Peggy (Katey Sagal) is the red-headed, sexually demanding wife of Al and mother of two. She has undertaken the career of home destroyer, bonbon binger and devoted mall maniac. Kelly, portrayed by the stunning Christina Applegate, is the man-friendly, blond-haired, blue-eyed teenage daughter of Al and Peg. Bud (David Faustino) is the perverted adolescent junior Bundy. Together, the chemistry of humour creates an atmosphere much like that of a good stand-up comedy team. They are one smooth delivery unit as their one-liners fall like dominoes in a row.

Together, they form the gruesome and not so wholesome foursome, the Bundys.

Critics do not take to it immediately because MWC doesn't follow the normal grain. Superstar TV families have been traditionally a white-collar conservative bunch. The Cleavers of Leave It to Beaver, the Bradys of The Brady Bunch, the Keatons of Family Ties, and the Huxtables of The Cosby Show are your typical upper-middle class success stories. The parents are role models, compassionate, and relatively secure in terms of dollars. The kids are mini-adults who just happen to experience the innocent frolicking of childhood. Pretty cut and dry stuff. Bobby finally finds the courage to ask his dream girl out. Wally decides to go to the same college as Daddy does. Jennifer decides not to cheat on the major test because it would be morally wrong. And so on and so on. But the Bundys are off the wall and refreshing. Peggy's bra maker discontinues her model in Illinois, so Al must cross state lines to replenish her supply. The couple participates in a game show where Al must be crushed by obese ladies under a mattress and Peggy is spun around on an upright "Wheel of Fortune" wheel. The kids ditch the parents at an expensive restaurant and take the family's meal money to catch a rock concert. This stuff is creative.

Family awareness groups have reservations about MWC. They are concerned that the graphic descriptions and racy issues might negatively affect the younger, impressionable audience. But the situations are laced with generous portions of humour and obvious exaggerations so viewers know it's purely meant as entertainment and not to try the stunts at home. Last season, though, a concerned mother began an intensive letter-writing campaign to contributing advertisers condemning the show. One episode was especially

targeted. Peggy mentioned that her toy vibrator was in the repair shop being "turbocharged." Coca-Cola blinked and pulled support from the show, fearing greater public outburst. Ratings rocketed as MWC was prominently advertised on print and video media. Little more has been heard from the protesters since, although the current season has cranked up the heat in a concentrated effort to surpass the first season's sly use of sexual connotations.

Katey Sagal has publicly defended the show and believes strongly in the right of television viewers to choose freely what they want to watch. Who's in control of the remote, anyway? If you are really bothered, channel hop from MWC to the news. What's more distressing? A lower-class family suffering another financial or spiritual setback or an escaped drug-crazed violent convict who has assaulted and killed innocent victims? Afternoon soap operas and all movie stations should be under similar attacks but are not. The power to press. The choice is yours.

The Bundys' state of wealth straddles the fine line

between poverty and an occasional feast of unrestrained
dining at McDonald's. In an era of spotlighting yuppie
wealth and materialism, one must realize the majority of
North Americans still live by the hair of their chinny-
chin-chins. Al with his hopeless home life fights for the
little guy largely ignored in the overhyped financial
feeding frenzy of the greedy eighties. It's time to look
back at the largely ignored 95 percent.

Married With Children is bold TV. It exists to fill a
new niche market which happens to be weary of the
much overused and abused "I love you, family"
facsimile sitcom. MWC exists to shock and make you
think. Think about how life may not be perfect for you
now, but there's always the Bundys. There are no
outrageous expectations for the characters. Life runs on
a exercise treadmill without an off button for them.
Plain survival and the wish for a better tomorrow are the
only hopes in life for the battlin' Bundys.

Hooray for first-class, kick-ass entertainment.

The Research Report

- people who are interested in getting information about a particular subject.

PURPOSE

- to present the facts in a compact, objective, easily accessible way.

LANGUAGE

- plain, formal, objective, and free of metaphor, rhetorical questions, personal anecdotes and the other techniques with which you often keep the reader's interest in an essay.

COMMENT

Essays and reports are similar; however information reports stress the facts rather than the writer's point of view. This example shows the structure of a basic report. It has several significant differences from an essay.

- The *beginning* consists of an informative title and a statement of purpose which replaces the thesis. There is usually no hook.
- The *middle*, while containing a series of paragraphs like the essay, has a heading on each main section.
- Where possible, visual aids such as graphs, charts, and tables summarize details in an easy-to-read way.
- For the *end*, the writer simply puts down the heading "Conclusion" and summarizes the main observations, findings, and results of the report.

This report shows an alternative to a title page. The information on author, teacher, course, and date can simply be put on the left hand side of the page one inch from the top. The pages are numbered on the right side, one-half inch from the top as shown.

Miranda A. H. Smith

Mr. G. K. Hamilton

GCA 2A1

9 October 1993

Push-Pull Factors in the Canadian

Immigrant Experience

PURPOSE

This report examines the factors which influence people to leave their country of origin and come to Canada. In order to carry out this study, 14 immigrants were interviewed at random from a community in Toronto, Ontario. These immigrants ranged in age from 25 to 73, and came from 11 different countries. All had immigrated between 1964 and 1988, with the majority (9) arriving in the 1960's. All responded in interviews to two questions: "Why did you leave your country of origin?" (the push factor) and "What made you decide to come to Canada?" (the pull factor).

IDENTIFICATION OF INTERVIEWEES

In order to protect the confidentiality of the interviewees, each was given a letter of the alphabet as identification. The following table shows county of origin and year of immigration of each of the people interviewed.

Table 1

Identification	Place of Origin	Year of Immigration
A	Columbia	1966
B	Columbia	1966
C	Ireland (Eire)	1988
D	Uganda	1972
E	Hong Kong	1968
F	West Germany	1964
G	India	1967
H	Hungary	1980
I	United States	1972
J	South Korea	1978
K	Guyana	1964

L	West Germany	1966
M	Guyana	1966
N	Pakistan	1966

THE PUSH FACTORS

Reasons for emigrating fell into four main categories. The Number 1 reason was a desire to further their education. Unstable political conditions and/or religious strife were also important. Three people mentioned a desire for adventure and "to see the world." A wish for improved economic conditions entered into the decision of only two people surveyed. Two interviewees gave reasons that did not fall into any of the main categories. One woman said she came out after her husband died because she was lonely and had "a good friend" in Canada. The other woman indicated that she did not want to stay in her homeland because she would have had "an arranged marriage with someone [she] didn't know."

THE PULL FACTORS

Immigrants to Canada picked this country for four main reasons. Most important was the influence of relatives and friends. In one case, a young boy came because his family brought him with them. In the other instances, people came because they already had relatives and friends in the country and these had recommended Canada as a good place to settle. Four people picked Canada because it was an English-speaking country; four mentioned job opportunities; and four thought that Canada offered superior education. Two people were drawn to Canada because of the medical plan and other social services. Four people mentioned miscellaneous reasons. The "low crime rate" was one. "Marriage to a fiance already living in Canada" was another. One person came because she "had studied about Canada in school." Finally, one man liked the proximity of Canada to the United States.

CONCLUSION

The conclusions of this report are best summarized in the following tables.

Table 2

Push Factors (i.e., those factors influencing departure from country of origin)

	A	B	C	D	E	F	G	H	I	J	K	L	M	N
Desire to further education	X	X								X			X	
Unstable political and/or religious situation				X				X		X				
Adventure				X								X		
Desire for improved economic conditions								X	X					
Other					X								X	

Table 3

Pull Factors (i.e., those factors influencing decision to come to Canada)

	A	B	C	D	E	F	G	H	I	J	K	L	M	N
Influence of relatives and friends	X		X	X	X								X	
English-speaking country	X	X	X	X										
Job opportunities								X	X	X			X	
Education					X				X				X	X
Social programs	X		X		X									
Other	X	X		X								X		

101